# CRITICAL /

MW00487870

# THE WORKS OF JAMES RADA, JR.

## Battlefield Angels

"Rada describes women religious who selflessly performed life-saving work in often miserable conditions and thereby gained the admiration and respect of countless contemporaries. In so doing, Rada offers an appealing narrative and an entry point into the wealth of sources kept by the sisters."

*Catholic News Service*

## Between Rail and River

"The book is an enjoyable, clean family read, with characters young and old for a broad-based appeal to both teens and adults. *Between Rail and River* also provides a unique, regional appeal, as it teaches about a particular group of people, ordinary working 'canawlers' in a story that goes beyond the usual coverage of life during the Civil War."

*Historical Fiction Review*

# Canawlers

"A powerful, thoughtful and fascinating historical novel, *Canawlers* documents author James Rada, Jr. as a writer of considerable and deftly expressed storytelling talent."

*Midwest Book Review*

"James Rada, of Cumberland, has written a historical novel for high-schoolers and adults, which relates the adventures, hardships and ultimate tragedy of a family of boaters on the C&O Canal. ... The tale moves quickly and should hold the attention of readers looking for an imaginative adventure set on the canal at a critical time in history."

*Along the Towpath*

# The Rain Man

"*The Rain Man* starts out with a bang and engages the reader with its fast-moving plot."

*Beyond 50*

"*The Rain Man* is a mystery thriller that races from the first raindrops that began the flooding to its dangerous climax in Wills Creek as it became a raging torrent."

*Cumberland Times-News*

# LOOKING BACK II:
## MORE TRUE STORIES OF MOUNTAIN MARYLAND

by
James Rada, Jr.

*To Karen & Bob,*
*Enjoy my look back*
*at western MD.*

## LEGACY
### PUBLISHING

A division of AIM Publishing Group

*James Rada Jr.*

To Robin Bosley,
my sister and friend
who could have imagined it?

Portions of this book were previously published in the *Cumberland Times-News, Maryland Life Magazine, Wonderful West Virginia Magazine* and *Allegany Magazine.*

LOOKING BACK 2:
MORE TRUE STORIES OF MOUNTAIN MARYLAND

Published by Legacy Publishing, a division of AIM Publishing Group.
Gettysburg, Pennsylvania.
Printed in the United States of America.
First printing: June 2012.

ISBN 978-0-9714599-6-0

Cover design by Stephanie E. J. Long

Printed in the United States by Morris Publishing®
3212 East Highway 30
Kearney, NE 68847
1-800-650-7888

Library of Congress Control Number: 2012907294

## LEGACY
**PUBLISHING**

315 Oak Lane • Gettysburg, Pennsylvania 17325

# Table of Contents

# How do you mend
# a broken heart?

One of the earliest pioneers in Allegany County never lived in Allegany County. Little is known about the man who is called the first white settler in Allegany County. He was English, his last name was Evart, he was heartbroken and he touches many residents' lives even today, nearly 260 years after his death.

In the early 18th Century, Western Maryland was part of Prince Georges County. Gradually sections of Prince Georges County broke off and formed their own counties. Frederick County formed in 1748. Washington and Montgomery counties broke off from Frederick County in 1776. Then Allegany County split from Washington County in 1789. Garrett County would split from Allegany County in 1872.

So it was into the wilds of Prince Georges County, not Allegany County, that a sad Englishman came to climb a mountain and be alone in his grief.

"While Col. Thomas Cresap is the best known early settler, Evart, heartbroken after being spurned by his sweetheart, turned to solitude in the savage infested wilds for a number of years before he died in 1749," the *Cumberland Sunday Times* reported in August 1955.

The only signs of Evart's existence were said to be a stone chimney about 10 feet high standing next to several apple trees high on a mountain.

"Local legend tells that in the 1730's Mr. Evitt (sic) moved to the wilds of Allegany County after suffering a disappointment in a love affair. He built a log cabin on the mountain and led a rugged, reclusive pioneer existence, never to marry. Some evidence of his early settlement remains on the mountaintop," according to the Maryland Department of Natural Resources web site.

The old home site is today part of the 3,000-acre Rocky Gap State Park. The park has a variety of hiking trails including one called the Evitts Homesite Trail. The five-mile-long trail virtually transports you back in time to Evart's day as you walk through Hemlock, Laurel and Rhododenron, cross a stream and then begin climbing Evitts Mountain. The trail climbs upward 1,000 feet over 2.5 miles.

As challenging as the trail is today, it was moreso in the early 1700's when Evart sought a place to escape from his heartbreak.

"His hope was to lose his identity and bury his name, but he failed for his name still remains on the Mountain where he lived," the *Cumberland Sunday Times* reported.

The 2,000-foot-tall Evitts Mountain is named in memory of Evart. At the base of the mountain is the 30-mile-long Evitts Creek, which takes its name from Evart as well.

For those who get their water from Cumberland's water system, you are drinking water from Evitts Creek.

*This article originally appeared in the Cumberland Times-News on May 5, 2008.*

# Where is General Braddock's lost gold?

Somewhere between Cumberland, Md., and Pittsburgh, Pa., a chest of gold coins lies hidden with what could amount to a couple million dollars in gold. It is buried beneath a tree at the confluence of two rivers according to the only survivor of the men who hid the chest from French soldiers and Indian warriors in 1755.

And yet no one has found it.

The fact and the legend, obfuscated by more than 250 years, have led treasure hunters for years to wonder "Where is General Braddock's lost gold?"

## Braddock's expedition

General Edward Braddock left Fort Cumberland on June 6, 1755, heading toward Fort Duquesne in Western Pennsylvania. The difficult terrain of steep mountain ridges and thick forests slowed their progress. Braddock's aide, George Washington, recommended splitting the army so that the best men could rush ahead and reach their destination while the rest of the army with the supplies would make its best time.

The gold was among the supplies. It was payroll money for the army. It would have also been used to pay Indians as guides and to keep them peaceful. Washington had brought it to Fort Cumberland from Williamsburg, Va., just before the army left.

When the army left Fort Cumberland is the last verifiable account of the gold.

A month later, the British were attacked by Indians working with the French. Around 500 soldiers were killed, another 500 wounded and just 300 survived without harm. Braddock was among the dead.

Only 28 Indians and Frenchmen were killed in the attack.

The gold was never seen again.

Indians working with the French attacked and killed General Braddock's men. The British troops were on their way to Fort Duquesne with a payroll chest, but buried it before they were massacred. Photo courtesy of the Library of Congress.

## Stories of burial

Legend says that before getting involved in the expected battle at Fort Duquesne, Braddock ordered the gold buried to keep it from the

French. The plan was to recover it after the battle was won.

Braddock held a council among his officers and asked them to wait until after the battle to get paid. They would not be able to spend the gold before then and because casualties were expected in the battle, there would be fewer men to divide the gold among after the battle.

The men agreed and six soldiers transported the gold to a location at the confluence of two rivers and buried the chest under a walnut tree.

Shortly thereafter, Braddock was killed and the remainder of the army retreated. No one ever returned to claim the gold.

## Becoming legend

A story recounted in *Incredible, Strange, Unusual...* by Harold Scott recounts a story from May 1881. A Cumberland man driving along the National Road, which was built along Braddock's army route, was about 30 miles west of Cumberland when he saw an old man holding a crow bar.

The man stopped his horse to watch the old man. The old man said he was a descendant of one of the men who had buried Braddock's gold. The story passed down through his family was that the chest was buried where a large rock divided two streams. Members of his family had been trying to find the gold since Braddock's defeat.

In October 1941, rain washed Allegany County for three days. After it ended, a hiker found a British coin on a road. The coin was close to a mountainside where water was still running off from the rainfall. Thinking the coin may have come from further up the mountain, the man began exploring and found another British coin. Though he searched for more on different occasions, the treasure eluded him.

Other rumors have appeared about the gold. In the 1950's, it was believed that the gold was buried where Crawford Run flows into the Youghiogheny River.

One story hypothesizes that the gold is still in Virginia in Fairfax County. Charles Gilliss wrote about his theory in 1954 that because Braddock was having trouble moving his men and supplies through Virginia's wilderness, he left some things behind. Among the items were two, small brass cannons that had been filled with gold and capped with wooden plugs. Gilliss said the cannons were buried "two feet beneath the soil, fifty paces East of a spring, where the road runs North and South."

**Six soldiers buried a chest of gold before being massacred along with General Braddock's troops. The location of the treasure is now the stuff of legends. Photo courtesy of the Library of Congress.**

One story hypothesizes that the gold is still in Virginia in Fairfax County. Charles Gilliss wrote about his theory in 1954 that because Braddock was having trouble moving his men and supplies through Virginia's wilderness, he left some things behind. Among the items were two, small brass cannons that had been filled with gold and capped with wooden plugs. Gilliss said the cannons were buried "two feet beneath the soil, fifty paces East of a spring, where the road runs North and South."

This account has been discredited, though, because Braddock and his army never came near the Centreville, Va.

Others believe that the French were able to recover the chest themselves and took it as spoils of war, though no one ever claimed credit for it.

*This article originally appeared in Lost Treasure Magazine in August 2011.*

# Windsor Hotel guest takes nighttime walk

The Windsor Hotel, which was built between 1842 and 1845 at the northwest corner of George and Baltimore streets, has had important guests over the years. A reception for President Zachary Taylor was held there in 1949. In February 1865, McNeill's Rangers kidnapped two Union General from Cumberland. One of them, Benjamin Kelley was staying in the Windsor Hotel, which was called Barnum House at the time. Two future presidents, Brigadier General Rutherford B. Hayes and Major William McKinley were both staying in the Barnum House at the time.

However, the hotel's most-unusual guest wasn't famous at all. S. S. Smith of Bedford, Pa., had had a rough day. He might have been stressed, tired or simply extremely fatigued. Whatever the reason, when he went to sleep in his bed in the room he was staying in the Windsor Hotel in September 1875, it was a troubled sleep.

The *Catoctin Clarion*, a newspaper in Thurmont in Frederick County, reported on a story in the *Cumberland Evening Times* that Smith "retired at night, and next morning awoke and found himself lying on the floor of an adjoining building." That building was the S. T. Little Jewelry Store building.

Smith had been sleepwalking. Though is usually strikes children, adults have been known to have the problem, too. The Mayo Clinic web site notes, "However, sleepwalking can occur at any age and may involve unusual, even dangerous behaviors, such as climbing out a window or urinating in closets or trash cans."

In 1875, a sleepwalker found himself on the second floor of the S. T. Little Jewelry store with no recollection of how he had gotten there. Courtesy of the Herman and Stacia Miller Collection and the Mayor and City Council of Cumberland.

It occurs during a deep, dreamless sleep even though the sleeper may have his eyes open. It can be caused by any number of factors, such as sleep deprivation, stress, fever, medications or sleeping in unfamiliar surroundings.

Though the reasons aren't known, Smith's sleepwalking may have been caused by trying to sleep in a hotel room rather than his own bed.

Once Smith returned to the hotel, an investigation was started to find out how he got from one building to the other without anyone seeing him leave the hotel. Sometime during the night, he apparently got up from his bed and climbed out his window or rather leapt from his window since there was no ledge and the roof of the Little building was six feet away. Then he walked along the roof and climbed in a second-floor window of the building.

"In making his way in he laid hold of a piece of wood loosely fastened in the wall, and it gave way precipitating him to the floor, the fall not hurting him, but thoroughly awaking him," the *Catoctin Clarion* reported.

Smith woke up astonished and not knowing where he was. It then took him an hour to find his way out of Little's building and back to the Windsor Hotel.

The Windsor Hotel eventually had a newsstand and barbershop on the first floor and was a part of downtown Cumberland until the building was demolished in 1959.

*This article originally appeared in Cumberland Times-News on December 26, 2011.*

# Frostburg firemen
# answer the call

When fire destroyed 40 businesses and residences in Frostburg on September 5, 1874, residents began thinking it was about time that Frostburg had its own fire company.

The fire had started in the loft of the Beall and Koch store on Union Street at 12:20 p.m. and it probably could have been contained to that building if a serious effort could have been made to drown the flames. It wasn't, though. Residents didn't have the ability to mount much more than a bucket brigade.

The fire quickly spread along Union Street, Broadway, Mechanic Street and Water Street. Keller's Store, Franklin Block, Marx Wineland's store and Hoblitzell Stables "being very dry structures, were in a few minutes a sheet of flames," according to the *Frostburg Mining Journal.*

A call for help went out, but the fire engines from Cumberland didn't arrive until 3 p.m. to put out the fire. Total losses from the fire were 40 businesses and homes totaling $149,900 (about $2.7 million today).

The damage from that fire that was caused by a delay in response started the citizens of Frostburg thinking that they needed their own fire company so they wouldn't have to depend on Cumberland's horse-drawn engines to arrive from 10 miles away.

And so, on March 18, 1878, a group of men met in the Frostburg city council chambers and organized themselves into a fire company of 35 members. George Wittig was named the first chief and George McCulloh was the first company president.

Though independently formed, the company expected the mayor and city council to help support the company with funds from the city treasury.

**Some of the firemen of Frostburg being honored during the annual Fireman's Parade in down Main Street. Frostburg's first fire company formed on March 18, 1878.**

The *Frostburg Mining Journal* printed some tongue-in-cheek advice to the new fire company members on Mar. 30. When the alarm sounds: "The moment you hear an alarm of fire, scream like a pair of panthers. Run any way, except the right way – for the furthest way around is the nearest way to the fire." Barn fire priorities: "Should the stable be threatened, carry out the cow-chains. Never mind the horse—he'll be alive and kicking; and if his legs don't do their duty let them pay for the roast. Ditto as to the hogs;--let them save their own bacon or smoke for it."

The following day, the company performed its first drill on the streets of Frostburg. The alarm was sounded at 3 p.m. and the men hurried to the hose house on Water Street from their homes around the city. The hose carriages were dispatched to the Gross and Nickel's furniture shop on Main Street where they were able to attach the hose to a fire plug and throw water within 4 minutes of the alarm.

On Apr. 6, the *Frostburg Mining Journal* announced, "Hereafter, in case of fire, the large bell in St. Michael's Church steeple will be tolled, instead of three being rung as for church related matters."

The company now had its manpower, equipment, hose house and alert system in place. One final administrative piece came on December 9, 1878, when the Frostburg Fire Department received its charter.

The Frostburg Fire Company has grown to two stations with more than 70 volunteers today who are on call around the clock to protect their families, friends and neighbors.

*This article originally appeared in the Cumberland Times-News on February 13, 2011.*

# Medicine shows always had something good for what ails you

The men stood on platforms so they were a few feet off the ground. That way, the crowds could see them and, more importantly, people could see the displays behind the men standing at the corner of Baltimore and Liberty streets in front of the Second National Bank in Cumberland. The men called out to the crowds. They cracked jokes, made sales pitches and overstated promises as they tried to sell homemade medicines.

On March 30, 1878, *The Alleganian* reported on the appearance of two worm medicine men who had "eloquence, stale jokes and slang phrases that have emanated from the street orators and wayside druggists. With stentorian lungs of wonderful endurance, they have shouted aloud, all the symptoms that indicate the presence of tape and all other kinds of worms that have ever afflicted humanity."

The men were convincing in their pitches because a majority of the crowds that gathered around them seemed willing to buy a bottle of the medicine. Part of their effectiveness was that the medicine men mastered the fear factor and convinced listeners that "every mother's son of them had from a quart to a half bushel of the parasites feeding upon his 'inward,' and others were satisfied that they had tape worms varying in length from thirty feet to thirteen miles."

Sickness was something that most people dealt with on their own at this time in Cumberland's history. The area had only eight doctors at this time to treat more than 11,000 people in the city, not counting anyone outside of the city limits. This created a ripe field for medicine men who promised easy answers to health problems.

**A salesman pitches his patent medicine to the crowd at a Missouri medicine show.**

As the years progressed, the shows became more refined and elaborate. By the 20th Century, the shows would set up tents on vacant lots in town and advertise their shows in the newspapers. The crowds would come to see the shows.

"Most of these medicine shows had Black musicians and entertainers, but the show would be directed by white owners," Herman Miller wrote in *Cumberland, Maryland, through the Eyes of Herman Miller.*

Once the crowd had gathered, the medicines were sold before the entertainment began.

Miller described a snake oil medicine show, which he calls, "One of the most colorful of all sellers of cure-alls."

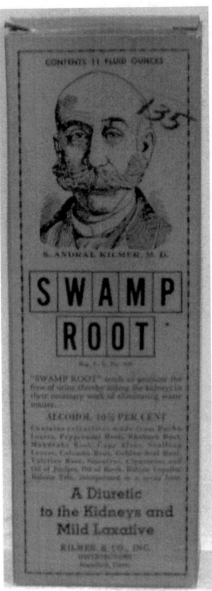

A bottle of Kilmer's Swamp Root promised to cleanse the body. It was one of the many patent medicines sold at traveling medicine shows. This bottle of medicine was sold around 1900. It is on display at the Edmonds (Wash.) Historical Museum.

A group came to town and rented a room in the building in that existed before the Fort Cumberland Hotel. The showmen keep rattlesnakes in a box that they would take out and drape over their necks and arms. The snakes were defanged, though not everyone realized this.

"The salesmen would then go to work telling all the benefits of rattlesnake oil. They were told the oil would cure everything from toothache to the common cold, bruises, sprains, skin diseases and other ailments," Miller wrote.

The cost for this miracle cure? A dollar a bottle.

Medicine shows died off as medicines became more regulated and getting healthcare from a doctor became easier.

*This article originally appeared in the Cumberland Times-News on February 26, 2011.*

# Presidential election hangs on the word of a county man

It's funny how history repeats itself. When President George W. Bush was running for re-election in 2004, he had to deal with a letter promoted by the Democratic Party that attempted to paint him as a hypocrite. The letter turned out to be a forgery that unraveled because of a simple mistake.

Bush was not the first President to face this kind of election trickery. In 1880, when President James Garfield was running for re-election, he had to deal with his own letter promoted by the Democratic Party that attempted to paint him as a hypocrite. And as with President Bush, the forgery unraveled because of a simple mistake.

And some of those mistakes were lies told under oath by a man from Allegany County who didn't exist.

On October 20, 1880, less than a month before the Presidential election, the *New York Truth* published its own "October surprise," under the headline "Garfield's Death Warrant." It was a letter supposedly written by Garfield to a man named H. L. Morey in Lynn, Mass. The letter was written on Congressional stationary and implied that the President supported Chinese immigration.

"Chinese immigrants accounted for a mere 0.21 percent of the U.S.

population, but politicians had effectively exploited the racism and xenophobia of many white Americans, especially in the West where most Chinese immigrants had settled. So volatile was the issue that both party platforms endorsed Chinese immigration restriction, and Garfield even highlighted the issue in his letter of acceptance," Andrew Gyory wrote in an article for the History News Network.

**President James Garfield**

The letter was a political bombshell that, if genuine, exposed Garfield as a hypocrite and threw his candidacy into question. The Democratic National Committee, which it turned out had been allowed to view the letter before it was published, quickly publicized it even going so far as to print up facsimile letters for distribution.

Party operatives distributed half a million copies in less than a week. They affixed posters of the letter on empty walls in town squares, hawked it on street corners, and handed out reprints to factory workers and school children. They even translated it for foreign-language voters and circulated badges featuring a grinning Mongolian, who smiles at the encouragement the Republican party gives him through its leaders," Gyory wrote.

Though President Garfield called the letter a forgery, he wasn't certain. He delayed his official response while his staff searched through his voluminous correspondence to a copy or some other indication of the letter.

Both Democrats and Republicans began collecting expert opinions on whether the handwriting was the President's or not. The postmark was studied. Investigators sought out H.L. Morey and were told that he had moved, he never existed or that he had died. Notices were placed in newspapers asking for affidavits from anyone who knew Morey.

The night before the election, the Democratic National Committee sent an affidavit to the press made by Robert Lindsay, a 19-year resident of Allegany County, Maryland. He had seen an ad in the *Evening Times* placed by William Price, head of the county's Democratic Committee. He swore that he had first met Henry L. Morey in 1874 and then had met him twice earlier that year.

The letter was widely printed and seemed to support the existence of Morey, who no one had been able to find. It appeared that Garfield's hopes for re-election were fading fast. Even if he could have responded to the affidavit, it wouldn't have been published until after the election. His political future lay in the hands of a fictitious man who was testify-. ing to the existence of another fictitious man.

## Will the real Richard Lindsay please testify?

Cumberland's nickname as "The Queen City" might have become "The Kingmaker" if a plan to influence the 1880 presidential election had worked. The revelation of the "Morey Letter," supposedly written by President James Garfield in his own hand showed the president to be a hypocrite on an important campaign issue. The letter had thrown what had seemed to be an easy re-election into uncertainty only weeks before the election.

Despite an exhaustive search for H.L. Morey, the recipient of the letter, he hadn't been found. Garfield had issued a statement saying the letter wasn't his, but officials with the Democratic National Committee across the country were saying that they were familiar with the President's signature and it was his.

Abram Hewitt, a U.S. Congressman and chairman of the Democratic National Committee, said in a speech, "some people may [might] incline to pronounce it a forgery. I have seen it. I am familiar with General Garfield's signature and I have compared it with his letters in my possession, and have no doubt it is genuine."

An investigation uncovered that the letter may have been written by Kenward Philp, an editorial writer for *The Truth*, the newspaper that published the Morey Letter, "who had long been known as a most able and dangerous imitator of handwriting," according to John Davenport in *History of the "Forged" Morey Letter*. Kenward Philp was charged on Oct. 27 and brought to trial in the hopes of reaching a decision before the election.

The Democratic National Committee refused to concede that the letter was forgery and continued looking for proof of its authenticity. The night before the election, the committee officials sent an affidavit to the press made by Robert Lindsay, a 19-year resident of Allegany County. He had seen an ad in the *Evening Times* placed by William Price, head of the county's Democratic Committee. He swore that he had first met Henry L. Morey in 1874 and then had met him twice earlier in 1880.

The affidavit was printed in papers around the country on the day of the election with no chance for the Republicans to respond until the evening papers, but by then a lot of votes had been cast. Garfield won, but not by the margin he had held before the scandal.

"Garfield won the electoral vote, 214 to 155, but the popular vote proved the closest in American history: Out of nine million ballots cast, Garfield surpassed Hancock by less than 2,000 votes (depending on which returns one accepts)," Andrew Gyory wrote in an article for the History News Network.

The letter "had beyond doubt cost the Republican candidates the electoral votes of California, Nevada and New Jersey. It was also quite clear to all careful observers of the political situation, that but for the evidence of the fraudulent character of the Morey letter, produced upon the examination of Kenward Philp, the forgery would have succeeded in electing the Democratic nominees," Davenport wrote.

The trial continued the next day with testimony showing how *The Truth* and the Democratic National Committee had worked together to present the letter in the most-damaging way possible. However, cracks in the case also began showing as some witnesses couched their stories in softer terms than they had used during the run up to the election.

Lindsay took the stand on Nov. 9. He said that he was a detective employed by "a secret organization of workingmen." He testified under oath that Henry L. Morey had been connected with Consolidated Coal Company's union. Morey and Lindsay had met for the last time between Feb. 4 and 10, 1880, when Morey had showed him the letter the letter from Garfield.

Col. Henry J. Johnson and Capt. William E. Griffith, both of Cumberland, had been investigating the specifics of the cased. When it came time for the cross-examination, they were ready. By the time they were through, they would show that Robert Lindsay, although he testified before them in court, did not exist.

## Cumberland man indicted for his part in plan to discredit President

Democrat leaders had put their reputations on the line before the 1880 Presidential election backing the authenticity of the Morey Letter, which was supposedly handwritten by President James Garfield and showed him to be a hypocrite. Allegany County resident Robert Lindsay had issued a sworn affidavit testifying that he knew H.L. Morey, the recipient of the letter. The affidavit gave those leaders additional support to try and discredit the President.

Garfield won re-election, if by a narrower-than-expected margin, and an investigation was started into the authenticity of the letter. This brought Lindsay's affidavit into question and revealed that not only was the affidavit false, but so was Lindsay.

When Lindsay took the stand during the trial in November 1880, he testified that he and Morey had met for the last time in February when Morey had showed him the letter from Garfield.

Col. Henry J. Johnson and Capt. William E. Griffith, both of Cumberland, had been investigating the specifics of the case. When they took the stand, the defense's case fell apart.

Robert Lindsay had not lived in Allegany County for 19 years as he testified nor was his name Robert Lindsay. He was James O'Brien of Washington D.C. William Price, head of the county's Democratic

Committee, had sent O'Brien to Cumberland before the election.

Price and a police officer named Birmingham had met O'Brien at the train station and began his instruction "in the role in which he was to play in this City in regard to the Morey letter. Birmingham taught him the story which he was to tell, took him to the prominent mines in the neighborhood, and tried to drill him into an exact knowledge of their locality and features, but as subsequent events proved, the time was too short, or the man too stupid, to gain sufficient knowledge of this kind to make a successful perjurer," the *New York Times* reported.

Lindsay was then sent to New York City where he was questioned in the trial to determine whether Kenward Philp, an editorial writer for *The Truth*, the newspaper that published the Morey Letter, had also forged the Morey Letter.

The *New York Times* noted that while in Cumberland, O'Brien had gone by the name of James Murray and in New York, he had called himself James Welch "so that he has had five names within a week."

Not only was O'Brien not Lindsay, he wasn't the first man used to play him and neither Robert Lindsay had sworn the affidavit issued under that name. DNC chairman William Barnum wrote the affidavit, according to O'Brien. The affidavit was then sent to Price in Cumberland, who had a man named O'Connery sign it before Price sent the affidavit to the press.

However, "On the night of the election O'Connery became drunk and roamed about the saloons of Cumberland, boasting of the affidavits that he had signed. It was evident that it would not do to send such a man here to testify," according to the *New York Times*.

So O'Brien was brought in to play Lindsay and testify in court. He was paid $10 when he arrived with the promise of $100 more when he was finished and on his way home.

Under cross examination, further evidence came out that the man who called himself Robert Lindsay was not who he said. He had said he had done an undercover investigation in the Eckhart coal mine while living with a lawyer named William Thompson on Baltimore Street. He also testified that he had taken the B&O Railroad from Cumberland to Frostburg.

# ADVERTISER EXTRA.

# GARFIELD'S DEATH WARRANT.

**That Letter in which he Advocates an Extended Chinese Immigration—He advises the Employers' Union of Lynn, Mass., "that the Question of Employees is only a Question of Private and Corporate Economy"—Read, Workingmen**

Herewith is presented a fac simile of the letter written by Gen. James A. Garfield, the Republican nominee for President, to H. L. Morey, of the Employers' Union, Lynn, Mass, and a fac simile of the envelope. Gen. Garfield has denied that he wrote the letter, and has asked Chairman Jewell to hunt down the author with detectives. It is also stated that the concelling stamp is one not used by the Washington, D. C., post office; something more than Garfield's word will be required to convince the public that he speaks the truth. [illegible] is not familiar. The concelling stamp is not used in the post office of the House of Representatives and not at the Washington, D. C., post office. The letter is true and expresses the sentiments of Garfield. Read, workingmen, and resolve to vote for Gen. Hancock, the honest friend of American labor.

*Personal and Confidential*

## House of Representatives,

*Washington, D. C., May 23, 1880*

*Dear Sir,*

*Yours in relation to the Chinese problem came duly to hand.*

*I take it that the question of employees is only a question of private and corporate economy, and individuals or companies have the right to buy labor where they can get it cheapest.*

*We have a treaty with the Chinese government, which should be religiously kept until its provisions are abrogated by the action of the general government, and I am not prepared to say that it should be abrogated, until our great manufacturing and corporate interests are conserved in the matter of labor.*

*Very truly yours,*
*J. A. Garfield*

*H. L. Morey,*
*Employers Union,*
*Lynn Mass.*

## THE ENVELOPE

The prosecution pointed out that there was no lawyer named William Thompson in Cumberland, the Eckhart Coal Mine had been closed for 12 years and the B&O Railroad did not go to Frostburg. Under questioning, it was revealed that O'Brien didn't know any of the Baltimore Street cross streets though he said he lived there. Though he said he worked in Eckhart Mine, he couldn't name any of the superintendents or foremen at the mine.

"It was evident to every person in the court room that the witness was a stupid, yet cool, deliberate and determined perjurer," according to the *New York Times*.

Though Philp was ultimately acquitted on charges of forgery, O'Brien and another man who had impersonated a relative of Morey's were indicted on charges of perjury and publishing false affidavits.

Though it was never discovered who actually forged the Morey letter, the revelation of the DNC's involvement to try and legitimize it for the same leaders who had been proclaiming the letter's innocence to issue a public apologize that was only reluctantly issued in order to avoid charges being filed against its members for their participation in the scandal.

*These articles originally appeared in the Cumberland Times-News in July, August, and September of 2011.*

# Lonaconing was a Phoenix rising from ashes of a devastating fire

It was a summer for Lonaconing in 1881. Even with the changing of the months from August to September and a cooling of the temperatures, there had been no rain for four weeks.

P.T. Tully and Co.'s store was on the east side of Main Street. On Sept. 7, Mr. Hanlon, one of the store's employees, was sitting down to a lunch with his family that would never be finished because a fire broke out in the stable behind the store.

The fire found fertile ground among the blowing wind, dry conditions and wooden structure. It moved to the store and then the flames began sweeping north along Main Street until there were no more buildings to consume and south to Bridge Street. The last building to burn was the Merchants' Hotel, kept by William Atkinson, who also kept a store adjoining the hotel.

With no fire department in town, people rushed to and fro with buckets of water trying to put out the fire and stop its progress. However, the dry conditions meant that water levels were extremely low. Calls for help went out and the Westernport Fire Department was the first on the scene within an hour.

"Fifty-three buildings went up in smoke in three hours. Overcome by panic, men broke open whiskey barrels and lay intoxicated in the street while the Westernport Fire Department put out the blaze," John Wiseman wrote in *Allegany County – A History*.

A Cumberland steamer arrived to help with the firefighting efforts, but the pump wouldn't work "and the Cumberland firemen, who were willing and anxious to do anything in their power, were obliged to return home after a short stay on the scene," John Thomas Scharf wrote in *A History of Western Maryland, Vol. II.*

"Had there been an engine of any kind in Lonaconing at the breaking out of the fire, much valuable property could have been saved. Fortunately, the principal loss fell upon those who were able to rebuild, although many lost everything," Scharf added.

This is Main Street in Lonaconing in the early part of the 20th Century. It looked different in 1881 before a major fire destroyed many of the buildings there. Courtesy of the Western Maryland Regional Library.

Among the buildings burned were D. R. Sloan & Company, Rechabite Hall, the German Lutheran church and parsonage, Dixon's Hotel (on Main Street), the Merchants' and Brady's Hotels (on Bridge Street), and Joseph Meyers' row of buildings on Bridge Street.

Firefighters were not without injury. James Carrigan, a tailor from Baltimore, located in Frostburg, had his arm cut off in jumping from the special train containing the Cumberland engine when it arrived at Lonaconing. David Dickson was badly burned from running through flames in order to save his own life. A falling joist burned James Hohing's wrist. Edward Lewis of Frostburg had his arm and neck burned. Robert Sommerville of Barton sprained his foot.

Men were put out of business and families left homeless in what was the biggest fire in the county in nearly half a century. The total loss covered 10 acres and was estimated at $150,000 and less than half of that amount was covered by insurance.

"Had the fire broken out at night there would have been a terrible loss of life, so rapidly did the wooden structures, which were built very close to each other, burn," Scharf wrote.

Despite the devastation of the fire, citizens rallied together and learned from their mistakes.

In the long run, however, the Lonaconing fire was a blessing.

Before the calamity the main street was a six-inch slough of mud for half the year, the long steps of houses ran to the streets, and there were no sidewalks. A year later the town organized a volunteer fire department, and a new sense of public-spiritedness, rekindled by a devastating flood in 1884, would lead to Lonaconing's incorporation in 1890, paved streets, and modern architectural touches," Wiseman wrote.

As a result, the Lonaconing Fire Company was organized in April 1882 with a hand pumper named "Minnehaha" and several hose reels serving as the first fire apparatus. In 1883, the first station was built, and in 1906, the organization changed its name to Good Will Fire Company No. 1.

*This article originally appeared in the Cumberland Times-News on February 8, 2010.*

# Show me the money!

Frank Laffin, a shoemaker, walked along the tracks of the Baltimore and Ohio Railroad near Cumberland on November 14, 1891, with two friends. The night was dark, making it hard to see where they were walking. The young shoemaker slipped as he stepped between cross ties and he fell through a cattle stop. His leg caught on something in the fall slicing Laffin's thigh just above his kneecap.

His friends pulled him up and off of the railroad tracks, but they couldn't do much for deep cut. The trio bound up the wound, but they knew by the amount of blood pumping out that Laffin needed to see a doctor and probably get stitches.

Laffin's friends helped him to a nearby home owned by C.H. Somerkamp. Somerkamp tried to bandage the wound, but he advised Laffin to get to a doctor for proper treatment. The problem was, Laffin explained, was that none of the men had any money to pay for a doctor. Somerkamp told them to go to Dr. William Craigen, who was the county physician. Since Craigen was in the county's employ and a doctor, he would take care of the injury whether or not Laffin had the ability to pay.

Dr. Craigen's office was at 19 S. Centre Street in Cumberland, according to a city directory. However, because it was in the middle of the night, the office was closed. Craigen's home was also in the same building so the men had woke the doctor.

Dr. Craigen looked at the wound, washed it, put two stitches in to close the wound and then bandaged the leg. Finished, Dr. Craigen told

Laffin that the cost of the treatment was two dollars and that he expected to be paid. The men explained that they had no money and couldn't pay the doctor.

Dr. Craigen said that unless he was paid, he would undo his work. Again, the men told him that they were penniless. "The doctor then leaned over the wounded leg, and with a pair of scissors, cut the stitches. Laffin's friends bandaged his leg as best they could and left the doctor's house," Herman Miller wrote in *Cumberland, Maryland through the eyes of Herman J. Miller.*

By the time the group reached South Centre and Williams streets, Laffin was in such pain that they had to stop at Ed Stanley's house. When another person at the home, A.H. Dowden heard what had happened, he fetched Dr. John Twigg, who came and replaced the stitches in Laffin's leg. Twigg then had Laffin taken to Protestant Home and Infirmary where the wound received more attention.

When news got out about Dr. Craigen's actions, the community was outraged. Even newspapers outside of Allegany County reported unfavorably on his actions.

"Dr. Craigen said the men were well dressed, and he thought they were well able to pay for his service, and he felt he sometimes had to stop impositions on the county," according to Miller.

The incident was investigated and Craigen managed to hold onto his position as county physician. However, he was discharged as a member of the Allegany County Board of Pension Examiners.

*This article originally appeared in the Cumberland Times-News on October 4, 2010.*

# Luke company was automobile pioneer, but nobody knows it

Before the town of Luke and before the Mead-Westvaco mill, there was the Maryland Automobile Manufacturing Co.

Little is known about one of the pioneering car manufacturers in the country.

The factory is mentioned in the book published by Luke during its 50th anniversary in 1977. The book also reprinted an old newspaper article about a woman who was searching for information about the steam runabout.

Charles Lowndes, J. Phillip Roman, Howard Dickey, Albert Dumb and Brooke Whiting began the venture with $10,000 in capital stock. A Mr. Pagenhardt was the chief engineer.

The factory was located on the lower end of Luke on what is now Cromwell Street. It was set up in the former Pagenhardt Bicycle machine shops.

The Maryland Steamer, a steam roundabout, was built from 1900 to 1901 and sold all over the nation. Their first delivery was in September 1900 when a racing car was sent to New York, according to Joe Weaver, vice president of the Allegany County Museum. They also had five more orders for delivery vans. Other vehicles were sold to customers in Pittsburgh.

The vehicles used a vertical two-cylinder steam engine and chain drive. The bodies were made of wood and filled with large-diameter, wooden-spoke wheels with solid rubber tires, according to the book, *Maryland Automobile History.*

At the time of operation, there were only three other steam-car manufacturers in the country. The company went into receivership a year later because the owners couldn't pay their bills.

Nowadays, no one remembers the factory. There are still two photos in existence of the factory, but apparently none of these classic autos still remains.

*This article originally appeared in the Cumberland Times-News on March 17, 2004.*

# City workers die in sewer line cave-in

November 9, 1900, was a Friday and certainly Nathaniel Rice and Isaac Foreman were looking forward to the late afternoon when they could relax and spend some of their pay. First, they had a full day of hard labor to get through.

They were part of the City of Cumberland work crews digging the trenches for the municipal sewer system. As people packed cities, waste disposal became a problem. If not properly disposed of, it created health risks and disease could spread easily through a dense population. The solution was a system of lines that could carry sewage out of the city usually to a river where it could be washed away to the sea.

When Isaac Foreman and Nathaniel Rice reported to work that morning, foreman Henry Martz assigned them to continue digging the ditch they had been working in the previous day on Arch Street near Sixth Street. The ditch was about 14 feet deep. Once the top soil was scraped off the ground, they had found themselves chipping away at soft clay. They would brace the sides of the ditch every few dozen feet as a safety precaution.

They were at their work place before 9 a.m. Foreman used a pick to break the clay loose while Rice shoveled the loose material out of the ditch.

"About nine o'clock Foreman noticed the earth above his head

33

trembling and with a cry of terror ran ahead for a place of safety near the brace. He nearly reached the point when the side of the bank gave way and buried him and his companion beneath tons of shale rock," the *Cumberland Evening Times* reported.

The cave in nearly filled in moments a stretch of ditch between two braces that had taken days to excavate.

Workers began shouting a warning about the cave in and anyone in the ditch further along quickly got out. Martz ran over to the spot and began checking off names as he saw the workers' faces in the crowd. He soon realized that it was Rice and Foreman in the ditch.

"While this silent roll call was being made 20 men were in the ditch working like mad to rescue their unfortunate companions alive if possible and if dead with as little delay as possible," the *Cumberland Evening Times* reported.

After about an hour of digging, the rescuers found Foreman's body in a stooping position. Perhaps he had tried to shield himself from falling debris or maybe the weight of the clay knocked him over.

"The life was crushed out of him and death was instantaneous," the newspaper noted.

Foreman's body was lifted out of the ditch and carried to Gangley's Hotel annex on Laing Avenue.

Rice's body was found about another hour later in a sitting position. He was "mangled and crushed almost beyond recognition," but his remains were also taken to the hotel.

The bodies were eventually transferred to the morgue of the Cumberland Furniture and Coffin Company. They were laid in coffins and buried a few days later.

Today, Cumberland's utilities workers own and maintain about 134 miles of water lines and 150 miles of sewer lines within the city, according to the city's web site. The old lines that Rice and Foreman gave their lives to dig a hole for have long since been replaced.

*This article originally ran in the Cumberland Times-News on January 30, 2011.*

# A century later, Pa. train accident relived

With Christmas just hours away, death was even closer for passengers on the Duquesne Limited, including 14 from the Cumberland area, in 1903.

A century ago, the Baltimore and Ohio Railroad's Duquesne Limited was the fastest passenger train running between Pittsburgh and New York. The 2-month-old Atlantic-type engine sped along at 65 mph pulling a baggage car, smoking car, day coach, six sleeper cars and a dining car.

Robert Davidson, a young salesman, was headed to Philadelphia where he was to be married on Christmas Day. He sat in the smoking car exchanging stories about his fiancee with Ambrose Good, who was on his way to New York to meet his fiancee. She was emigrating from London and they were to be married on Christmas Day as well.

In all 150 passengers were aboard the train December 23, 1903. The smoking car was so full that people stood in the aisles.

The engine rounded a sharp curve just west of the bridge over James Creek around 7:45 p.m. Lying on the tracks in front of the train were six switch ties—railroad ties that are heavier and larger than typical ties. They had fallen off Gondola No. 3087 as it had gone around the turn earlier in the evening.

With no time to stop, the Duquesne Limited hit the ties and derailed. The engines left the tracks toward the left while the rest of the cars went off toward the right, ripping up rails as they did. The train's momentum kept it moving forward for some distance even after it left the rails. As the engine toppled, the tender was thrown into the air over the boiler and landed ahead of the rest of the train. The baggage car rolled over the embankment and stopped near the Youghiogheny River. The dome of the locomotive pierced the side of the smoking car, breaking off as it did.

Once the cars stopped moving and the sound of tearing metal ended, a new sound filled the air. The broken locomotive dome was venting live steam from an engine that had been running at full speed and the steam was spewing into the smoking car, boiling the passengers trapped inside.

Passengers and crewmen who could free themselves from the wreckage, grabbed axes, sledges or any available tool to try and break into the smoking car and free the dying passengers.

Their efforts were hampered when a fire broke out in both the day coach and smoking cars.

Conductor Lewis Helgoth managed to crawl out of the wreckage only to realize he was dying. While he was part of the present emergency, he knew there was an even greater tragedy looming that he couldn't do a thing about in his condition.

Then he saw Baggage Master Thomas Dom staggering alongside the wreckage. Dom was nearly blinded by blood from a scalp wound but he could walk.

"I'm scalded to death. For God's sake, get a red lamp and flag 49 or she'll be on us," Helgoth said.

The No. 49 train traveled the same tracks behind the Duquesne Limited and would be only minutes behind. Just as the Duquesne Limited hadn't seen a problem on the tracks because of the sharp turn in the track, neither would the next engineer be able to see a problem in time to stop.

Dom staggered to the rear of the train, searching for a lamp as he went, but he couldn't find one that wasn't smashed.

He thought desperately for something to do that would warn the No. 49. He dug his matches out of his pocket and pulled his coat off. He lit it on fire and waved it in the crisp December air.

The No. 49 engineer was Moses Johnson. He saw the flame moving back and forth, cutting through the darkness. Then he realized the flame was over the tracks. Someone was trying to warn him of something. He applied the brakes as fast as he could without derailing the train. Even so, the No. 49 had been traveling at 55 mph. It slid to a long and slow stop.

All the while, the flame, and the danger it warned of, grew closer. Johnson first recognized the man holding the flaming coat and then he saw the wreckage behind Dom.

Johnson closed his eyes and prayed the train would stop in time. He could do nothing more.

The No. 49 stopped three feet from the back of the wreckage with Dom in between them. When he saw the No. 49 was safe, he let out a sigh and fainted.

Porter D.W. Hills hobbled to the smoking car immediately after the crash and helped with the rescue efforts of the passengers who were being burned by fire and water.

Hills said, "The car was the most awful scene I ever witnessed. Men were jammed in all sorts of shapes. They were on top of each other and buried under heaps of dirt and seat cushions. When I tried to lift one man out, I found others so tightly wedged into the same place that several had to be aided at the same time. Baggage and clothing were scattered all around. Here and there were little piles of toys and other Christmas gifts."

When Davidson was pulled from the wreckage, he told the doctor who unsuccessfully tried to save his life about his fiancee. Then he said, "Write to her, doctor. Tell her I was brave—my last thoughts were of her."

In all, 65 people died in the wreck.

# 14 from Cumberland area died about passenger cars

Here are the local people who died in the wreck of the Duquesne Limited:

**George Biser** – A 22-year-old lineman with Western Union who lived in Berkley Springs, W.Va.

**William J. Coakley** – A 30-year-old glassblower who lived on North Centre Street in Cumberland. He left behind a wife and three children. He had been working in Rochester, Pa., and was on his way home for Christmas.

**Harry Devlin** – A 30-year-old fireman for the B&O Railroad. On the night of the crash, he was a passenger on his way home to visit his parents in Lonaconing for the holidays.

**William H. Edwards** – A 25-year-old resident of Frankfort, W.Va., who was on his way home to his wife and a family reunion on Christmas.

**Lewis Helgoth** – A conductor on the train who helped avert a larger disaster. Helgoth's friend Baggage Master Thomas Dom was with him when he died. Dom said Helgoth whispered his goodbyes to family and friends, groaned lightly, and then rolled on his side away from him and died.

**John William Ketzner** – He lived on North Centre Street with his parents (he was 19 years old). He worked as a Western Union telegraph lineman. He and his family had moved to Cumberland in 1901 from Harpers Ferry, W.Va.

**John K. Powers** – A 47-year-old glassblower who had been working in Rochester, Pa. He lived on North Centre Street in Cumberland and left behind a wife and five children.

**J. William Martin** – A 35-year-old telegraph operator from Hancock who left behind a wife and two kids.

**Martin Sheedy** – A 35-year-old widower from Patterson Creek, W.Va., employed with Bennett and Talbot.

**Brant W. Smallwood** – A 28-year-old news agent who lived on Maryland Avenue in Cumberland. He left behind a widow and one child.

**Joseph Schellhouse** – A 29-year-old glassblower who had been working in Rochester. He was engaged to marry Margaret Himmler and was a candidate for the Democratic race for the Maryland House of Delegates.

**William Thornley** – An engineer on the train who lived in Hazelwood, Pa.

**Charles W. Wagon** – A 29-year-old resident of Berkley Springs, W.Va. who left behind a wife and two kids.

**John Wills** – A 28-year-old machinist from Mount Savage.

*This article originally appeared in the Cumberland Times-News on December 23, 2003.*

# A Frostburg hero to the rescue

French writer and dramatist Romain Rolland once wrote, "A hero is one who does what he can. The others don't." He must have known Frostburg's J.J. Mealing.

Alfred Croft had brought his one-horse sled over the mountain from his Garrett County farm and into Frostburg to deliver a load of hay. It was January 18, 1907, and Union Street (now Main Street) was snow covered, making the sled the preferable way to travel.

After finishing his errands in town, Croft turned the sled westward and headed back toward Big Savage Mountain. Along the way, a half a dozen school children piled on the back to enjoy the sled ride up the street. A short time later the ride became more of an adventure than an enjoyable jaunt.

"Something frightened the horse; he took the bit in his teeth, broke it and ran wildly up-street. At Broadway a passenger car added to his scare and he plunged madly out that street," reported the *Frostburg Mining Journal* in 1907. The *Mining Journal* was Frostburg's best-known newspaper published from 1871 to 1919.

Croft remained fairly calm as the horse charged forward. He tried to regain control of the horse, but pulling on the reins had no effect since they pulled on a broken bit, which hung outside the horse's mouth.

39

The horse's hoofs threw snow backwards as it plunged forward in the harness, pulling the sled along in its panicked run. In the back of the sled, the children remained oblivious to their danger and just enjoyed the ride.

**Frostburg's Main Street in the early part of the 20<sup>th</sup> Century. Courtesy of the Albert and Angela Feldstein Collection.**

Bailiff J. J. Mealing was standing at the corner of Mechanic Street and Broadway talking to Thomas Shea when he saw the wild horse racing toward him on Broadway. He could see the children laughing in the back, but more importantly, he noticed that Croft's exertions on the reins were having no effect.

"Comprehending in an instant their peril, at immense risk to himself he met the animal in the street, grabbed it by its nostrils, and although slung up and carried off his feet some distance, he held on and finally brought it to a standstill," according to the *Frostburg Mining Journal.*

Regaining his feet under him, Mealing straightened up and attempted to keep the horse calm. While Croft explained what happened to the horse and thanked Mealing, Shea caught up with the group.

When he saw the broken bit, Shea hurried to his nearby home and brought back a bridle for the horse. With the new bridle and bit, Croft would be able to drive the sled back to Garrett County.

Croft and Mealing helped the children off the sled. They were disappointed the ride was over, but they had never realized the danger they were in. Bystanders had realized the danger, though, and attributed the safe conclusion to Mealing's quick actions and willingness to face danger.

"Hence, if ever a man deserved a life-saving medal, Mealing in this instance won several," wrote the *Frostburg Mining Journal*.

*This article originally appeared in the Cumberland Times-News on September 17, 2007.*

# The crazy clubs
# of Cumberland

Allegany County has its fraternal and civic organizations, the Shriners, Lions, Moose, Red Man and others, but none was quite so unusual as those fraternal groups from the early 20th Century.

In 1909, John Rhind of Cumberland told a group of men in Lonaconing who were members of The Only Great Club about a new fraternal group in the county called the Veteran Bachelor's Association founded in November 1909. Jerry Kean served as president.

"The club is not a month old yet and I am the father of it," Rhind said in *The Evening Times*. "No man is admitted who is less than 70 years old. We want no young bucks. We want season veterans, who have reached the age of discretion, and who are no longer in danger of succumbing to the wiles of the artful widow or the desperate old maid. Our membership at present is 37, and we are not anxious for a large membership."

The motto of the club was stated to be "We hate them," though it remained unclear as to whether that referred to wives or women in general. The members pledged themselves to discourage matrimony in every legal way possible.

This pronouncement of the Veteran Bachelor's Association caused one person in attendance to compare it to another unusual Allegany County club called the Misfit Club.

"No, there is only one Misfit Club, and the capers of that organization would make a horse laugh," Walter Clark said in *The Evening Times*.

As an example of their hi-jinks, Clark said that the club had planted a barrel of clams at the bottom of the canal with the hopes of raising them. However, when a diver went down to check on them later, it was discovered the clams had all migrated to an empty beer barrel and the crop was a failure. Presumably, the clams must have gotten drunk and died.

This led Semmes Devecmon, who was in attendance to proclaim that "Cumberland was full of freaks, individual and organized. The Misfit Club was composed entirely of loons; the newly composed Bachelors' Club was composed of sour old cranks," according to *The Evening Times*.

"I can name you half a dozen societies in Cumberland in which there is not a single member who is all there, mentally," Devecmon said.

However, almost as if to show that Cumberland did not have a lock on slightly daft, Harrison Fazenbaker of Lonaconing stood up a short time later and recited a short poem about complainers.

"When things get all kertwisted
An' the wrinkles on your brow
Makes you look as sour as thunder
An' ye can't tell why or how
Jest remember fret an' stew
Has laid some good men on the shelf
An' ye'll join 'em if you worry
So wake up and hump yourself."

"That's all I've got to say this evening," Fazenbaker said.

But he wasn't done. Following a poem by another member about dry towns in West Virginia, Fazenbaker got up to share another poem about the North Pole.

One can only assume that while the towns in West Virginia may have been dry, these club meetings certainly weren't.

*This article originally appeared in the Cumberland Times-News on January 6, 2010.*

# The B&O's Christmas gift to Cumberland

As Christmas 1909 approached, it was looking like it would be a merry one. The country had come out of a weak economy. Retailers were seeing strong crowds in their stores.

Then on Dec. 6, *The Evening Times* announced, "Cumberland's Christmas gift from the B. & O. is to be a handsome, modern passenger depot of artistic design, which will cost $100,000."

While the popular Queen City Hotel had been a jewel in Cumberland's crown for decades. The Baltimore and Ohio had built the Italianate-style hotel designed by Thomas N. Heskett beginning in 1871. It was completed the following year. It was both a station for train to stop and a destination spot for tourists. It had more than 100 rooms, a formal garden with a fountain, billiards room and a grand ballroom. Railroad hotels were needed at the time because George Pullman had not yet invented the sleeping car.

It was a tourist destination for people looking to escape the stifling summer heat of placed like Washington D.C. and Baltimore.

"People would come [to Cumberland] on trains; trains were big in the 1860's and so forth," Ed Mullaney said in *Cumberland: A Hometown History*. "There were nine passenger trains a day that would come through the B&O Station and ... many people would get off and stay in Cumberland. Cumberland was a good dropping off point [to] take a rest."

Though the plans for the new passenger station weren't announced until December 1909, they had been around since 1906. According to *The Evening Times*, Division Engineer Leighty and his assistants draw up the plans in the summer of 1906, but it was shelved because the economy was weak.

The new passenger station would take up three floors. The first floor area would include men's and women's rooms, baggage storage, women's retiring room and ticket office. The second and their floors would include engineering and general offices. The passenger entrance to the passenger station would be on Park Street. The construction / renovation didn't actually begin until 1911 and it was completed in March 1912.

**The Baltimore and Ohio Railroad built a modern station onto the Queen City Hotel that opened in 1912 that included a large waiting room, smoking room, reading room, emigrant room and offices. Courtesy of the Library of Congress.**

The first ticket was sold to E. W. Marquis to travel to Roberts Station on No. 5 train which left Queen City Station at 5:20 p.m. on March 24, 1912. *The Evening Times* described the complete station this way:

"The entire first floor is given over to the comfort and convenience of passengers. The waiting room is 64 x 43 feet and contains the ticket office and news stand and is paved with red tile. To the rear of the large waiting room are a smoking room for men and a reading room for women.

"The basement floor is given over to an emigrant room and two room adjoining are arranged for trainmen.

"The second floor of the building contains the main office of Division Superintendent Hoops and the clerical force, equipped with new furniture, and steel lockers for the use of the force. The telegraph office for official business is on the floor beneath.

"The third floor is taken up with offices for the working forces, such as the division engineering, claim agent, trainmaster of the Connellsville division and others."

Over the years, the Queen City Hotel and Station would host such guests as President Ulysses S. Grant, Buffalo Bill's Wild West Show and Assistant Secretary of War George D. Meiklejohn.

At the time, it was one of the last remaining railroad hotels and the new passenger station had been the only major renovation to the building during that time.

*This article originally appeared in the Cumberland Times-News on November 29, 2009.*

# No. 20 mine explosion kills 23

The ground trembled around 8:30 a.m. on the morning of April 24, 1911. Some people in Elk Garden, W.Va., might have wished it was an earthquake, not that the town had ever experienced one. But that was better than thinking about the alternative. There had been an explosion in the nearby Davis Coal and Coke Company No. 20 mine where most of the men in town worked.

People ran from their homes and hurried toward the mine to see what had happened, and more importantly, if anyone had been injured or killed. "Many of those who stood round the slope heading were parents, brothers, sisters or wives of those entombed and great feeling was shown, many wringing their, hands and crying aloud, while others, the more courageous, set about planning means of rescue," reported the *Cumberland Evening Times*.

The nearby town of Thomas was notified and sent two fire engines with rescue crews to Elk Garden on the Western Maryland Railroad. A count was taken of the miners who had exited the No. 20 mine. Twenty-seven were missing. Only five have been able to make their way out of the mine.

The men working in No. 20 had left for their shift at 6:30 a.m. Work had slacked off during the winter and the miners were only working two days a week. That made it tough going financially for the Elk Garden miners so when the chance had come to work an extra day, they had made sure not to be late. Even so, it wasn't a full shift. The men who had been called into work were cleaning up the mine in preparation for the next day's work.

A crowd gathers around the No. 20 mine in Elk Garden awaiting word on the fate of the coal miners trapped inside after an explosion collapsed part of the mine. Courtesy of the Kitzmiller Mining Museum.

Superintendent Robert Grant organized a rescue crew from the men in town, most of them miners themselves. The rescue crew entered the smoking mine, hoping for the best. Though Grant knew where the men had been working, he kept running into passages closed by falling coal. They snaked their way through passages until they got as close as they could to where the miners working at the time of the explosion had been.

People from town brought bolts of bed ticking and cloth to build temporary bratticing for the rescue crews so that air could flow into the mine. All of the actual brattice in the mine had been blown out by the explosion.

Many of the wives and children of the trapped miners returned to their homes, trying to keep their hands and minds occupied with thoughts other than they were now widows and their husbands had died horrible deaths.

As word of the explosion spread, men began arriving from other areas to help with the rescue efforts. A large group of men from Thomas, WV, was one of the first on the scene. Davis and Coal Coke Company officials notified the Department of Mines in Washington so that a rescue car could be sent to help.

"Work was then begun, making a cross cut through the wall of coal towards the entombed men. Gas still lingers very heavy in the mine and work is possible only at short intervals, and then the strain on the rescuers is terrific," the *Cumberland Evening Times* reported.

In fact, four rescuers themselves were overcome with the gases in the mine. They were pulled from the mine and treated for afterdamp, which is left in a mine after a fire or explosion. Afterdamp is a gas mixture made up of primarily of nitrogen and carbon dioxide. It can suffocate a person is he inhales too much of it.

At 3,000 feet into the mine, the rescuers dug towards the miners not knowing whether they were dead or alive. By evening, it was estimated that the rescue crew was about halfway to the room where the miners had been working. "As the way progresses the work grows harder and the prisoners will probably not be reached until tomorrow afternoon," the newspaper reported.

Monday evening, a body was found. He was identified as Wilbur Shears. A few hours later, near midnight, five more bodies were found. They were loaded onto wagons and driven into Elk Garden where a temporary morgue had been set.

The grieving began, but there still remained hope, though fading.

When the Department of Mines' rescue car arrived late in the evening, it brought with it oxygen helmets to protect the rescuers against afterdamp. They were instructed on how to use the helmets safely. The helmets allowed the rescuers stay in the mine longer in their search for the missing miners.

During the day on Tuesday, nine more bodies were found and then another five in the evening. "Some of the dead were burned about the face and hands, some were bruised and faces scarred, while others showed no external signs of violence, but seemed to be calmly sleeping," the *Piedmont Herald* Reported.

At noon on Wednesday, the final three bodies were carried out of the mine. The wait was over for the families, but now the search for what had happened would begin.

## Why did the No. 20 mine explode?

Their wives had waited in their homes, trying to ignore the clamor going on just outside their doors in late April 1911. They had busied themselves cooking and cleaning and all the time praying that what they could feel in their hearts was not true and was simply stress making itself known.

An explosion in the Davis Coal and Coke Company No. 20 mine in Elk Garden had trapped 23 men behind tons of rubble in the shaft. Men from all over the region were racing to get to the miners, but removing the debris that clogged the shaft took time.

The *Piedmont Herald* reported, "In giving credit for heroism displayed in rescue work at the mine we do not wish to detract any credit due the many faithful mine officials, but we do wish to commend the miners of the Elk Garden region, including Wabash, Oakmont, Kitzmiller, and from distant mines for their coolness, still and daring. It was their brother miners entombed and they toiled, they braved the dangerous gases, they reeled under the influence of the poison and when refreshed plunged into the mines again."

Unfortunately, heroes aren't always successful. Knocks on doors began being heard late in the evening of April 24. Even those who could not hear what was said recognized the sobs of a grieving wife. As each body was pulled from the rubble and each widow notified, the hopes of the remaining wives fell.

"The women in nerely (sic) every case staid (sic) at home and there patiently bore the awful suspense until their loved ones lifeless forms were brought to them by the undertaker. It is difficult to tell which were the greater heroes, the women remaining at home in deepest grief, watching, hoping, praying, or the miners braving the deadly gases to rescue the bodies of their unfortunate comrades," the *Piedmont Herald* reported.

Despite the fact that mining deaths were almost commonplace, "never before has there been a mine disaster in that region that paralleled, or even approximated the shocking calamity last Mon. morning, when twenty-three men, all citizens of Elk Garden, except one, were suddenly ushered into eternity by an explosion in Mine No. 20, which is owned and operated by the Davis Coal and Coke Company," reported the *Mineral County News Tribune.*

According to a Department of Mines annual report, only 25 men died in mining accidents during the year ending June 30, 1911, and 23 of them had died in Elk Garden. The average age of the 23 miners was 31 with the youngest being 18 and the oldest being 57 years old. These weren't inexperienced miners, either. Among them, they averaged 13 years of experience.

Five of the miners were buried on Apr. 26 and the rest of them on the following day. "The undertakers did their parts exceedingly well, and worked on almost exact schedule time. The congregations gathered quietly and quickly, and while one interment was going on in the cemetery another funeral was being held in the church," the *Piedmont Herald* reported.

The Davis Coal and Coke Company paid all of the funeral expenses for the miners. In addition, the company had also taken out $400 (around $2,200 today) of life insurance for each of its miners, which the widows received. All of the widows were also given goods from the company store to make sure that their immediate needs for food and other necessities would be met.

Once the funerals ended, the questions began. "The dead are buried. The ghastly scenes that will remain in our memories while life shall last are now in the past. The heart still aches but submits to the awful stroke, and feels that some day we shall understand," the newspaper reported.

The cause of the explosion was believed to be an accumulation of gas and dust in the mine. Because of the infrequency of work, the mine had not been running for days when the miners went into the mine on Monday morning. It was something that would have to be investigated.

The West Virginia Department of Mines opened hearings into the mine explosion in early May. As officials questioned various experts and witnesses, they came to the conclusion that the explosion hadn't been caused by a natural gas leak because the mine should have been wetted down, which would have minimized the risk of coal dust igniting. As dust, coal has a lot of surface area that provides plenty of opportunity for a spark to take hold. Once a spark does catch, it creates a domino effect that spreads quickly.

Chief Laing of the West Virginia Department of Mines announced at the end of the hearing, "The evidence gathered, the chief states, seems to point to the breaking of the mining law by their miners, who are thought to have used black powder."

The coroner's jury met for two days and was able to determine what happened even more precisely. The jury's conclusion was that a blown-out charge had been fired by James Pugh or his son, Arthur. This caused the coal dust to ignite, which led to the explosion.

The miners killed in the explosion were: James Brown, 38; William Buskey, 25; James Dempsey, 57; Leo Dempsey, 23; Samuel Hamilton, 25; Ed Harshberger, 33; William Hetzel, 40; Hawthorne Patton, 20; William Pearson, 32; Arthur Pritchard, 18; John Pritchard, 48; Frank Pugh, 29; William Pugh, 24; Walter Runion, 20; William Sayres, Jr., 30; Wilbur Shears, 31; Harry Tranum, 26; John F. White, Sr., 42; John White, Jr., 24; Charles Wilson, 21; John R. Wilson, 57; Lester Wilson, 18; Roy Wilson, 23; Tom Wilson, 23, and Tom Yost, 29.

*These articles originally appeared in the Cumberland Times-News on April 2 and 30, 2011.*

# Labor Day was a time for parades in the Queen City

Hundreds of people gathered at Park Street on Monday morning, September 7, 1914.

Organizers rushed back and forth, trying to put the right people in the right places, which was quite a feat when the line of people stretched out for nearly a mile.

At 10 a.m., the three bands in the parade line struck up their songs and the first people in line began to move out along Park Street as the Labor Day parade began.

Labor Day had been a national holiday since 1894, and thousands of Cumberlanders turned out each year to honor their union workers, such as glass workers, bakers, miners, plumbers and carpenters.

"The day was ideal for marching, and every local paraded full strength, some uniformed in white and carrying souvenirs in miniature of their handicraft," reported the *Cumberland Evening Times*.

Allegany Trades Council President John Carbrey served as grand marshal of the parade and he was assisted by Col. Charles Roemer, Charles Danner, Clarence Shinholts and William Allamong.

A platoon of police officers led off the parade with Police Chief Eisenhauer leading the way.

Cumberland Mayor Thomas Koon, members of the city council, county commissioners and judges of the orphan's court rode in cars in the leading section of the first division of marchers.

"Among the features of the parade was a monster American flag that completely filled the width of Baltimore Street. It took at least 50 men of one local to keep the four sides of the flag taut in the September breeze," reported the *Cumberland Evening Times*.

The flint-glass workers local was headed up by 200 boys who each carried ornamental glass canes. In all, 30 locals had members representing them in the parade.

**The Footer Dye Works float in a Cumberland Labor Day parade during the early part of the 20th Century. Photo from the Herman and Stacia Miller Collection courtesy of the Mayor and City of Cumberland.**

Cumberland tribes of the Improved Order of the Red Men also held a place in this Labor Day parade because their own parade in August had been rained out. "Also a cavalcade of mounted 'braves' and wagons full of 'papooses' who enjoyed and enlivened their portion of the parade," reported the newspaper.

The floats that displayed the different trades followed the Red Men.

From Park Street, the parade marched down Baltimore Street to North Mechanic Street to Centre Street to Bedford Street and disbanded at City Hall.

The events of the day moved on to the Labor Day picnic at Narrows Park. Attendees had a variety of entertainment including speeches, amusement games, sports, band concerts and dancing. The amusement games included a sparring contest, a pole-climbing contest, an egg race for girls, a potato race for boys and a shoe race for boys.

All in all, it was a day of fun enjoyed by the entire family.

*This article originally appeared in the Cumberland Times-News on September 6, 2004.*

# The new business was "smoking" hot

The doors of 121 Baltimore Street had been closed for more than a month in 1914. Many people thought the bowling alley that had occupied the space had gone out of business and they were right. However, V.T. Wolford and his son were set to open something new and better in the business space.

On September 3, 1914, the *Cumberland Press* announced that a new club called, The Smoke Shop, "will throw open its doors this evening as the finest cigar store and pocket billiard room in the state."

The bowling alleys were gone and in their place were five of the finest pocket billiard tables available. As for the cigars, "The management has endeavored to place in their store every known brand of high-grade cigars, tobacco and cigarettes and have adopted as their motto for this department, 'We dare you to ask us for something in our line that we haven't got.'," according to the *Cumberland Press*.

The interior had been redesigned and painted by a popular Baltimore decorator at the time named Herman DuBrau. DuBrau had been born in Prussia in 1865 and graduated from the Royal Arts Academy in Berlin, Germany, as a "Master of Arts." He emigrated to Baltimore in 1892 with his wife and two daughters where he embarked on his career as a mural artist and decorator, who added his touch to many of the public buildings in Baltimore.

The doors to the club opened at 6:30 p.m. on Sept. 3 and by evening's end, more than 1,500 people had passed through. This is an even more-astounding number when you consider that The Smoke Shop was a gentlemen-only club.

**Cumberland's Baltimore Street near where The Smoke Shop opened in 1914. From the Herman and Stacia Miller Collection and courtesy of the Mayor and City of Cumberland.**

"Many of these were traveling men and they were high in their praises, saying that 'The Smoke Shop' is the finest billiard room in the state," the newspaper reported the following day.

Wolford gave away cigars as souvenirs to commemorate his store opening.

While such stores are rare today, in the early part of the 20$^{th}$ Century, they were quite common. Herman Miller wrote in his book *Cumberland, Maryland through the eyes of Herman J. Miller* that downtown Cumberland had four cigar and tobacco stores and five pool rooms in 1910. By 1930, that number had risen to nine cigar and tobacco stores and five pool rooms.

*This article originally appeared in the Cumberland Times-News on September 5, 2010.*

# Foul ball!

During the 1915 baseball season in Allegany County, you might have seen two games being played on the same field...at least if the teams playing were the Midland Peppers and the Frostburg Demons. The rivalry between those two teams in the Georges Creek and Cumberland Baseball League was so intense that it wasn't uncommon that when the two teams met on the field, other things would happen besides a baseball game.

The baseball season in Frostburg kicked off on May 6, 1915, with a parade that crowded Main Street. Businesses, which had all been decorated for the celebration, were closed from 2 p.m. to 5 p.m.

"As the parade started, one looking up Main street could see nothing but a mass of people on the curbs as far as the flat," the *Allegany Citizen* reported.

The grand celebration brought around 3,000 fans out to the ball park to see the opening game. However, even before the game, there were hints at how intense the rivalry was between the two teams. Rumors had been going around that Midland was going to bring in ringers for the game to ensure a win. The Midland team, of course, denied the accusation, saying they could win with their regular roster.

The game was a crowd pleaser. It lasted two hours and went 11 innings before a winner emerged.

It was not without its controversy. In the eighth inning, the crowd left the bleachers and flooded the field in their excitement. "Even the women took part, and when Midland refused to continue the game until the field was entirely cleared they proceeded to engage with a wordy war with several members of the Midland team," the newspaper reported. When the crowd didn't return to their seats, Manager Alcott with the Peppers filed a protest.

In the end, the Demons prevailed with a 7-6 win.

The rivalry between the two teams didn't diminish over the summer and the two teams met again on August 30, 1915. This time, the game was to be played at the Midland Athletic Park.

**Sports rivalries have always found fertile ground in Allegany County. One such rivalry was between the Frostburg Demons baseball team and the Midland Peppers. Courtesy of the Frostburg Museum.**

Charlie Dye was pitching for the Peppers, but he was also a former Demon and his teammates were more than familiar with his pitching techniques. They quickly pounded their former teammate for four hits and four runs.

"The Demons went into the game with lots of ginger and kept it until the last man was out," the *Allegany Citizen* reported.

The Demons handed the Peppers "a drubbing," according to the paper.

As the Demons took a 4-1 lead in the third inning and added another run in the fifth, the second game began. Midland didn't score its run until the second inning and they didn't get their next run until the eighth.

In the fifth inning, Peppers' Manager Poland handed the umpire, a man named Small, a protest.

"It was filed on account of Johnson who signed with Lonaconing in the first of the season. He was playing under the name of Mellon," the newspaper reported about one of the players on the Demons.

Not only that, but the Peppers also found Small's umpiring unsatisfactory "as the players were wrangling with the official the entire game. One time the Midland team left the field and threatened to stop the game," according to the newspaper.

The game was eventually finished with Frostburg also winning the second time by a score of 7-3.

The Cumberland and Georges Creek Baseball League was one of many leagues that sponsored baseball games in the early decades of the 20th Century. Some of the teams participated in more than one league. The other teams in the Cumberland and Georges Creek Baseball League were the Cumberland Colts, the Piedmont Drybugs and the Lonoconing Giants.

*This article originally appeared in the Cumberland Times-News on June 1, 2009.*

# You ought to be in pictures

Could Cumberland have been Hollywood? It certainly has the mountains where a large "Cumberland" sign rather than "Hollywood" could have been mounted. It once even had a movie studio looking to locate in the Queen City.

Around the same time when Hollywood was becoming home to Nestor Studio, Cumberland also had its chance at celluloid immortality. The first feature filmed in Hollywood was *The Squaw Man* directed by Cecil B. DeMille and shot in 1914. However, the city's future as the center of American filmmaking was not yet secure.

O. F. Malcom with the Titan Film Company had passed through Cumberland months earlier and had liked what he had seen in the Queen City. He returned to Cumberland in early September 1915 for "possible establishment of a branch of the organization here, filmed a number of well-known people and scenes while here and made in all about 105 feet of film," reported the *Cumberland Press*.

This time Malcolm came with H. R. Olson, a cameraman with Titan Films. The amount of film shot would have totaled about 3 minutes by best estimate. The plan was to show the shot film the following week in a Cumberland theater.

"Cumberlanders will then have an opportunity to see some people they know and some scenes that they will recognize, as well as a sample of the work done by these operators," the newspaper reported.

Olson used a French camera from the J. Debrie Company in Paris. It cost over $1,000 and was considered one of the best movie cameras of its day. The Debrie Parvo camera was one of four such cameras in the country at the time because World War I had ended all exporting from France. The camera was contained in a wooden box with a hand crank on the side. It could hold 120 meters of film.

**This is a Debrie Parvo camera, which was used to film scenes in Cumberland for a possible motion picture.**

On Sept. 9, a crowd quickly gathered near Cumberland's city hall and the fire engine house to watch the filming. Both the chief of police and the fire chief were called on participate in the filming. "The men were instructed to 'act' and both proved good actors," the newspaper reported.

Police Chief J. Thomas Eisenhauer approached Fire Chief Willison on the street. The two men shook hands and began to talk casually. Not an exciting scene, especially when viewers would not hear the conversation between the two men.

The next segment showed "Baldy" Enochs, Cumberland's oldest firefighter at the time, sitting at the station. The fire alarm sounds and firefighters rush to their posts. The trained fire horses hurry to take their place at the front of the horse-drawn fire engines. The firefighters climb on board the engine and start out of the station to save the day.

Fade to black. Roll credits.

There's no word on audience reaction when they viewed the film. Nor is there any record about whatever became of the Titan Film Company. Although Cumberland and Western Maryland never became Hollywood, they still remain popular places to shoot many television specials, movies and documentaries.

*This article originally appeared in the Cumberland Times-News on August 9, 2009.*

# Plane makes emergency landing in Elk Garden

Nowadays, the sight of a plane flying overhead is no big deal, but it wasn't always that way. The Wright Brothers made their historic flight at Kitty Hawk, N. C., in 1903 and Charles Lindbergh flew non-stop across the Atlantic Ocean in 1927. In between, planes and their pilots were a rarity.

Coal miner Kenny Bray wrote in his unpublished memoirs, that whenever a plane did fly overhead, "it was a big attraction. Very few people had ever seen a plane up close."

One day, in September 1920, that changed for the people of Elk Garden, W.Va., and many of the surrounding coal towns. On Sept. 14, a crowd had gathered in Elk Garden to watch a baseball game between two coal town teams when a plane flew in from the northeast.

"It was flying low, apparently in trouble," Bray wrote. "It tried to land on the ball field, but the crowd scattered out all over the field and it could not land."

It stayed in the air and continued flying until it landed in a field owned by the Saul Stullenberger in Elk Garden. "In landing, the plane turned over but neither occupant was injured. The machine was much damaged," the *Cumberland Evening Times* reported.

The crowd from the ball field followed the plane's flight and surrounded it when it crash landed.

Two men, whose last names were Burdo and Seagraves, had been flying from Mineola, N. Y. to Pittsburgh, Pa. They had landed in Cumberland to refuel. However, after they left, they lost their way in a dense fog and developed engine trouble. Their predicament in Elk Garden was the result.

The men made repairs to the plane and tried to get it started again. Bray said that the plane had "what appeared to be a radiator on the front with the propeller on a shaft that came through below or near the bottom of the radiator." To start the engine, one of the men turned the propeller by hand. The newspaper identified the plane as an Italian S. V. A.

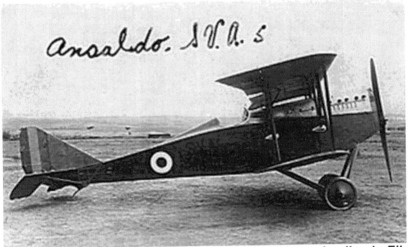

**This is the model airplane that made an emergency landing in Elk Garden in 1920. Courtesy of Wikimedia Commons.**

"Then the two men stood in front of and to one side of the plane," Bray wrote. "The man nearest the plane grasped the right hand of the man with his left hand. They then ran by the plane and [the] man nearest the plane gave the propeller a twist as they ran by. They did this a few times until the engine started."

The men climbed back into the plane and took off. The plane got off the ground, but it still wouldn't fly properly. The plane landed a second time, though this time it was done right side up.

The plane was dismantled and Howell Keplinger used his team of horses to carry the parts into town. From there, the plane parts were packed up and shipped away on the Western Maryland Railroad for replacement or repair. Burdo accompanied the shipment to New York to get replacement parts.

When he returned after a few days, he and Seagraves made repairs to the plane, which took another day or two. Once done, the men started the engine, got in and flew off into the sunset.

*This article originally appeared in the Cumberland Times-News on March 4, 2012.*

# Cumberland takes off

On May 17, 1922, Cumberlanders looked into the sky, pointed and to quote a famous comic book said, "Look, up in the sky. It's a bird. It's a plane. It's..." Well, actually it was a plane and if not the first one to fly into Cumberland, it was the most-important one.

Army Lt. Paul Wilkins and mechanic George Baker landed a DeHavilland DH-4 Army airplane in town at Cumberland Heights and Oldtown Road. The site is behind St. Mary's Catholic Church on Prince George Street, according to Bob Poling and Bill Armstrong in their book, *Wings Over Cumberland: An Aviation History.*

There they were joined by Cumberland resident A. Hammond Amick, Jr. The trio took off and flew over the Lamp Farm, Mexico Farms, Mapleside, Potomac Park, the Amcelle area, the Vale Farm near Frostburg, Vale Summit and the Welton Farm. It wasn't just a joy flight. The men were searching for a place to build an airfield.

Since planes in 1922 couldn't fly the long distances that modern planes can, refueling stops were needed along air routes. One of those air routes was between Bolling Field in Washington D.C. and Wright Field in Dayton, Ohio. Cumberland made a nice midway stop.

"Former aviators of this area, it was reported, have planned extensive activities for the proposed air field here. It is likely that one or two planes will be purchased by aviators and housed at the landing field. Also planned is the erection of a light tower on one of the mountain tops near the city for the purpose of guiding night flyers," the *Cumberland Daily News* reported.

Planes of the era had little cross-wind capability so they needed to land directly into the wind. This meant that early airfields did not have runways. They were literally large fields that allowed planes to approach from any direction and land into the wind. The aviators liked what they saw at Mexico Farms and recommended it as the site for the airfield. However, leasing the field for the asking price of $250 per year proved too cost prohibitive for the U.S. Army Air Service.

Rather than lose the opportunity to bring planes and aviators into Cumberland, the Cumberland Chamber of Commerce set to work to develop a workable solution. The answer was announced in a telegram from Maj. Gen. Mason Patrick to Amick. "Will lease for nominal sum of one dollar per year from chamber of commerce allowing gas and oil concession to be given by the chamber," Patrick wrote.

Mexico Farms was first listed as an official Government Landing Field in the September 15, 1923, issue of the *Aeronautical Bulletin*. Maps of the air field appeared on the first page of the bulletin.

"The city of Cumberland donated services in the preparation of the field, and in November 1923, published that the field was available for visiting aircraft," wrote Poling and Armstrong.

By 1924, two 80-foot radio transmission towers and a gravity-fed refueling station were built at the air field. The Army Quartermaster Corps constructed a barracks and operations building to house five soldiers stationed at the air field.

During its long history, Mexico Farms Air Field has hosted many famed aviators, including Wiley Post, Charles Lindbergh, Howard Hughes and Gen. Billy Mitchell, but most notable is that it was a stop on the first around-the-world flight in 1924. Lowell Thomas wrote about the six-month journey in *The First World Flight*. Three planes left Washington D.C. on September 13, 1924, heading toward Ohio. After leaving Mexico Farms Airfield, the group ran into fog so thick, that the escort planes were forced to turn back, though the main plane managed to find its way through.

Today, Mexico Farms Airfield is still in operation and is the second-oldest air field in Maryland.

*This article originally appeared in the Cumberland Times-News on October 5, 2009.*

# 1922 railroad strike became a matter of life and death

It was an accident waiting to happen; one that some people were probably hoping would happen because it might get them a larger salary.

The country was entering the fifth month of a nationwide railroad strike in August 1922. The Railroad Labor Board had announced that it was cutting wages by seven cents an hour, which led the shop workers to strike, though they were the only railroad work group that did so. Still, there were 400,000 shop workers on strike, including 1,400 who worked for the Baltimore and Ohio Railroad and the Western Maryland Railway in Cumberland.

It was the largest railroad work stoppage since 1894 and it became bitter. The railroad companies brought in 300,000 strikebreakers to fill the vacant positions. Violence began escalating so that by the end of July, the National Guard was on duty in seven states and 2,200 deputy U.S. marshals were carefully watching meetings and picket lines.

When a proposed settlement by President Warren G. Harding failed, people began to realize that the strike might last for some time.

During the strike, Western Maryland Railway trains began experiencing problems. Air hoses were cut, switches misapplied and car journals were sanded. Railroad officials reported that there had been hundreds of these incidents in the two months of the strike.

The cut air hoses presented a dangerous problem. The hoses weren't cut all the way through so that they burst when the trains tried to brake. Usually this meant the car had to be removed from the train and taken onto a sideline where it could be repaired.

"It is possible that a serious derailment might have occurred from these sources, causing loss of life of passengers and crew," reported the *Cumberland Evening Times*.

In one instance, the Al G. Barnes circus train had its journals sanded and hoses cut, but the sabotage was discovered before the train left Cumberland. Even so, the train was unable to leave the city before the repairs could be made putting the circus well behind in its touring schedule that season.

The Western Maryland Railway hired the Burns Detective Agency to find out what was going on. The detectives investigated and photographed employees sabotaging the trains without them knowing it. Railroad officials identified the employees as striking employees some of whom had been with the WMRR for years.

The men were shown the pictures during their disciplinary hearings right before they were fired.

Despite the convictions, the Western Maryland Railway still remained on alert for sabotage. "Every freight and passenger train is carefully guarded from such criminal acts as far as possible, it was stated, before they are dispatched from terminals now," the newspaper reported.

The strike continued until September when an agreement was reached. At that time, strikebreakers began resigning their positions as the B&O Railroad hired back its shop men. In some instances in South Cumberland, strikebreakers "were stoned, and chased and struck with dinner-buckets and forced to run in various directions. Several resented this and free-for-all fights occurred, including a dog fight, in the street during the fracas. Several of them were badly bruised and beaten," reported the *Cumberland Evening Times* on September 19, 1922.

The Western Maryland Railway was more reticent to rehire, in part, perhaps from the amount of loss that the railroad incurred because of the sabotage.

*This article originally appeared in the Cumberland Times-News on June 4, 2011.*

# Cars and sleds begin sharing the streets

By 1923, cars were no longer a novelty on Cumberland's roads. They had surpassed horse-drawn wagons and carriages as the main form of transportations. With more cars on the streets, the chances of accidents rose.

Cars could zip along at speeds of 40 miles an hour or more. However, just like today if a driver tried to stop too quickly on snow-covered streets, the car could slide out of control.

That was causing problems because children sledding shared a similar problem. Once their sled was in motion, it was hard to stop. Unfortunately many of them didn't stop until they hit a moving car.

This led parents to action. At a city council meeting in February 1923, "The suggestion that a special street for sled riding by children be roped off and protected by city authorities in order to prevent accidents from vehicular traffic was frequently heard today," reported the *Cumberland Evening Times.*

The initial program began with the police department barricading a few selected streets in the city on snow days and allowing sledding in the evening from 7:30 p.m. to 10 p.m. Using any other city streets could get you arrested, according to a 1926 *Cumberland Evening Times* article.

The program grew in popularity. More streets and Constitution

Park were added for sledding. The Cumberland Recreation Department and then the Parks and Recreation Department became the administrators of it.

**When the snow fell in Cumberland in years past, the city would block off certain streets to allow sledders to have fun on the city's hills without danger of being hit by a car. Photo from the Herman and Stacia Miller Collection courtesy of the Cumberland Mayor and City Council.**

"We would put barricades out and lanterns on them at the top, bottom and main intersections with the street," said Gene Mason, a former director of the Cumberland Parks and Recreation Department.

The *Cumberland Evening Times* noted that the streets were left unplowed to allow one night of sledding. At the most, streets were barricaded 36 hours. Following the night of sledding, the barricades were removed and the streets plowed and had cinders spread on them.

Mason said he even enjoyed sledding with his children. His last time sledding was in the late 1960's when he was sledding on Winifred Road with his daughter. His daughter was riding down the hill on his back when they hit a bump and went into the air. When they came down, the sled's runners folded under them.

"She went flying through the air," Mason said. "I slid a few feet and scratched my face. I also cracked two ribs. My daughter thought it was great fun and wanted to go again. I told her, 'You can go, not me.' It was hurting me to breathe."

By the 1970's, 19 streets in seven sections of the city were being set aside for a day of sledding. This didn't stop kids from sledding at other locations, but problems that arose only supported the need for the sledding program. In 1967, the *Cumberland News* reported on a number of children injured in accidents with cars when they were sledding on streets not set aside for sledding.

"I don't recall any complaints about the program by the neighbors," Mason said. "They recognized that it provided a safe place for kids to sled."

Mason said the program ending in the city in the 1980's.

"You just don't see as many kids riding sleds on the city streets now," Mason said. "It was a good program, though, and the kids enjoyed it."

*This article originally appeared in the Cumberland Times-News on November 29, 2010.*

# Footer's formula for success began in English textile mills

Thomas Footer knew the formula for wealth. He was a chemist after all. You take one part a good idea and add to it eight parts of determination and one part belief in yourself.

It was a formula that had worked for him. He was born in England in March of 1847. His father was a papermaker, but "He lost both parents in early childhood and began to earn his own living as a boy," according to the *Cumberland Evening Times*.

The way he chose to earn his living was to work in the textile miles of England and Scotland where he learned about dyes. During this time, he didn't neglect his studies, going to night school to learn more about the subjects related to his chosen profession. One of those courses was chemistry, which he studied in depth.

He married Elizabeth Booth in England in 1866 and three years later, they emigrated to America. According to the *Cumberland Evening Times*, Footer spent a "short time with Jobe woolen mills near Berkeley Springs before coming to Cumberland."

He opened his dye works business in a small workshop on North Liberty Street doing all of the work himself. As with many small businesses, it was hard to make ends meet in the early years, but Footer was a tireless worker and determined to make a better life for him and his family.

"In 40 years from the small workroom Mr. Footer saw his establishment go into a large plant covering a wide acreage, with nearly 1,000 skilled employees in its various departments," the *Cumberland Evening Times* reported.

He used his knowledge of chemistry to create better dye formulas. He also invented several appliances and machines that had specific applications to his business. He maintained a lab in his plant where he studied fabrics, washing compounds, dyes and mixtures.

"As an employer of labor he was always known to be fair, reasonable and appreciative, and in the creation of the extensive plant that bears his name he designed in every way for the comfort and contentment of the workers," according to the newspaper.

**Thomas Footer, fifth from the left in the back row, was a member of the Cumberland City Council in 1894. Photo from the Herman and Stacia Miller Collection courtesy of the Cumberland Mayor and City Council.**

His reputation in business grew so that Footer Dye Works was known throughout the East with branch operations in many cities. The business also came to be worth several million dollars.

Even as his net worth increased, Footer did not flaunt his wealth publicly. However, he did travel widely for business buying art and rare books from the places he traveled. In public, though, he was an unassuming man "with a strong aversion to notoriety."

This aversion to notoriety didn't stop him from serving his community, though. At different times, he served as the president of the Maryland Theater Company, on the executive committee of the chamber of commerce, director of Liberty Trust Company, Junior Grand Warden of the Grand Lodge of the Masons of Maryland and Exalted Ruler of the Cumberland Lodge of the Benevolent Order of the Elks. He also served on the Cumberland City Council as a councilman, president of the Cumberland Board of Trade and he even ran for mayor.

As Footer aged, he stepped back from his business duties and eventually sold control of the company to a syndicate, but he remained the chairman of the board.

His health remained good until the final year of his life. Early in 1923, Footer traveled to Battle Creek, Mich., to undergo treatments at a sanitarium there. His health was reported as improving only days before his death.

Then on August 21, 1923, he passed away leaving behind his wife, three sons and two daughters.

*This article originally appeared in the Cumberland Times-News on February 6, 2012.*

# Neighborhood came to boy's recue

One moment, 7-year-old Keith Pirkey ran along playing with his friends on a pleasant evening in March 1925.

In the next moment, he was gone, vanished in a puff of smoke. Only it wasn't smoke but a small cloud of dust.

"Keith!" Charles Smith, a playmate, called out.

He had seen his friend disappear and it frightened him.

"Help!" came a muffled reply.

Charles moved toward the voice slowly, wondering how Keith could have vanished and yet Charles could still hear voice.

Keith's voice grew louder and Charles looked down. He saw the hole in the ground that was barely wider than him. It had been dug for a telephone pole.

Charles knelt down by the hole. A dirty, tear-stained face looked up at him.

"I fell in," Keith told him.

Charles didn't know how deep the hole was but Keith's head was about 2 feet below the top of the hole. Charles draped his arm into the hole.

"Grab it," he told Keith.

Keith shook his head. "I can't. My arms are stuck at my side."

"I'll get your father."

Charles ran off, first making a stop to tell the other boys he and Keith had been playing with what had happened. By the time Charles returned to the hole with Herman Pirkey, the boys had gathered around the hole to look at Keith.

Herman grabbed his son by the shoulders and pulled him up. Keith rose a few inches before he caught tight in the hole. Keith yelped in pain.

"What's wrong?" Herman asked.

"My knees are pinching against the side," Keith told him.

"Unbend them so I can pull you out."

"I can't; there's not enough room. I can't move them."

Herman knocked his head against the ground in frustration.

"Don't worry, Keith, I'm going to get some help," Herman said.

"Dad, I'm scared. It's hard to breathe."

Herman ran back inside his home at 634 Hill Top Drive and called the police. Before too long, Assistant Chief of Police J. P. Minnick, Officer John Smallwood and Edward Wilson, a telephone company employee, arrived.

Wilson saw the hole and asked, "Why wasn't that hole covered?"

"That doesn't matter," Herman said. "How do I get him out?"

By now a crowd had begun to gather around the hole. Herman, Wilson and the police pushed their way through the crowd to examine the hole. They decided that the only way to get Keith out was to dig him out.

They put a sack over Keith's head to keep dirt from falling in his face and mouth and propped an electric torch between his chest and the wall of the hole so that they could see what they were doing.

Wilson drove off and returned shortly with picks and shovels. The crowd quickly snatched up the tools and dug a slanting trench around the boy that widened the hole.

Keith suddenly waved his arms, showing they were free.

Moments later, he was able to straighten his legs.

Keith was pulled out of the hole and into the anxious embrace of his worried father. He was uninjured and simply scared, cold and a little wiser about watching where he ran.

*This article originally appeared in the Cumberland Times-News on April 26, 2004.*

# Fire threatens
# Allegany Hospital

On March 30, 1925, someone struck a match. By itself, it wasn't an act worth noting. It happened thousands of times a day in Cumberland back then. This person lit his cigarette or maybe a pipe and then gave the match a quick shake so that the flame would go out. Then he tossed the spent match aside.

This is one possible explanation for the beginning of what happened that day, but not the only one. No one knows who lit what with what and then threw it aside to start the fire. All that is known is that a match or something else on fire fell down a waste chute and that it wasn't extinguished.

The flames ignited a pile of paper and cloth at the bottom of the chute in the furnace room. Those flames smoldered sending smoke up through the metal-lined chute and from there, it spread throughout the first floor of Allegany Hospital on Decatur Street.

"Although many of the patients became frenzied with excitement, they were soon calmed by the scores of doctors and nurses who hurried to the hospital when they learned of the fire," wrote Herman Miller in *Cumberland, Maryland through the eyes of Herman J. Miller.*

The hospital had 65 patients at the time who needed to be evacuated from the hospital. Four infants and three maternity patients were carried across Decatur Street to the home of Charles E. Mullan.

Someone phoned in the alarm and the East Side and Central fire companies in town responded to the call. In addition, the hospital had its own fire extinguishers that were used to put out the flames before the firemen arrived. The firefighters searched the hospital and found where the fire had started in the furnace room. They determined that there was no further danger and returned to their stations.

The patients began returning to their rooms and staff began mopping up the water used to extinguish the fire.

"It was then discovered that a fire more intense than the original one was bursting through the chute doors," Miller wrote.

The fire had made its way into the wooden joists and lathe behind the walls. Finding a new source to feed the flames, the fire grew. A new alarm call went out and this time all four of the city's fire companies responded.

ORIGINAL HOSPITAL

**In 1925, a carelessly discarded cigarette started a fire in Allegany Hospital that caused the evacuation of the hospital. Courtesy of the Albert and Angela Feldstein Collection.**

Flames began breaking through the walls at various points. The firefighters used their axes to tear away portions of the wall and floor to get at the flames with water. It took them several hours of feeling walls and floors for heat and sniffing out sources of smoke until they were convinced all of the flames were out.

By that time, the smell of smoke was prevalent throughout most of the hospital. Some patients wanted to leave the building. Others were moved to a wing of the hospital where the smell didn't reach.

The damage was significant but fire insurance covered the costs. Repairs were made and business at the hospital continued.

Allegany Hospital would continue to grow at its Decatur Street location. It was built as a 25-bed facility in 1905, but by 1913, two years after the Daughters of Charity took over the hospital administration, it had tripled in size. A five-story annex would be added to the hospital in 1936.

The name of Allegany Hospital changed to Sacred Heart Hospital in 1952 and it moved from Decatur Street to Haystack Mountain in 1967.

*Update to the story:* After this article ran, Donald Keene called me. He's was an 85-year-old Lonaconing resident who was a baby when the fire at Allegany Hospital occurred. He was about a week old at the time. "My mother always told me that I was such a firecracker that I started the fire."

*This article originally appeared in the Cumberland Times-News on May 3, 2010.*

# Honoring home team loyalty

Allegany County has always loved its sports teams, but it's not often you hear about how much the athletes on those teams loved Allegany County.

In the early part of the 20$^{th}$ Century, sports in Allegany County were just, if not more, intense than it is nowadays.

"Almost every town of any size boasted its own baseball team. Intense rivalry marked the games between towns; it was almost a certainty there would be a fistfight or two to add to the excitement," Harry Stegmaier, Jr. wrote in *Allegany county – A History.*

The Cumberland Colts was Cumberland's minor league ball team from 1916 to 1932. The team began in the Potomac League, and then moved to the Blue Ridge League, but from 1925 to 1932, the Colts were part of Mid-Atlantic League and, for a time, a farm team for the New York Yankees.

In 1926, catcher Mike Thompson's contract was sold to a team in Scottsdale, Ariz., but Thompson didn't want to leave Cumberland. He liked the town and he liked playing baseball in the Queen City.

"Thompson went to the limit when he refused to report to Scottsdale and stayed with Cumberland. He drew a $100 fine out of the controversy that was raised while his case was being settled and he therefore became the property of the Colts at a loss of that much cash," reported the *Cumberland Evening Times.*

By declaring himself the property of the Mid-City Baseball Association, the owners of the Colts, Thompson threw himself and the team into expensive litigation that ended in early June 1926 when the National Board of Arbitration of Baseball Clubs denied the Scottsdale team's hold on Thompson and he was allowed to remain the property of the Cumberland Colts.

**Baseball has long been popular in Cumberland. The city had a minor league team called the Cumberland Colts that was a farm team of the New York Yankees. Photo from the Herman and Stacia Miller Collection courtesy of the Cumberland Mayor and City Council.**

Following the decision, fans began looking for a way to honor Thompson's loyalty and to help him defray the costs of his fight to stay in Cumberland, which had cost him hundreds of dollars.

The *Cumberland Evening Time*s reported that Thompson "since joining Cumberland has made all the difference in the world in the work of the team and promises to be a valuable man to the club through the years."

The decision was made to play a double header at Mid-City Baseball Park on June 13. The admission price for the games would be increased by 25 cents with the extra quarter going into a defense fund for Thompson.

Mid-City Baseball Park had been built in 1923 on Wineow Street near the Chesapeake and Ohio Canal wharves. It had a seating capacity for 6,000 and parking spaces for 300 cars. The stadium contained wooden grandstands and was surrounded by a wooden fence. No grass grew on the field. Baseball was played on a dirt lot. The design was modeled after a stadium in Newark, N.J.

On game day, 3,000 people showed up, which means that $750, more than enough, was raised to pay Thompson's legal expenses to stay in Cumberland.

The Colts played the Uniontown Cokers and split the games. The Colts won the first game 7-5 and the Cokers won the second game (which was called in the seventh inning on account of darkness) 3-0.

Thompson donned his Colts uniform and took his place behind the plate on June 14 for another game against Uniontown. He had two at bats and scored one run, but the Colts still lost the game 8-5.

Nonetheless, it was a victory for Thompson who was playing for a town that he loved and a town that loved him.

*This article originally appeared in the Cumberland Times-News on August, 13 2007.*

# National pastime deadly for local residents

The team may have been amateur, but the baseball game on July 8, 1928, was considered excellent. St. Patrick's of Mount Savage were the current leaders in the Holy Name Baseball League, which was made up of church teams in the county. St. Patrick's team came to Frostburg on July 8 expecting to win, which they did. However, they encountered unexpected resistance from the team from St. Michael's Catholic Church in Frostburg team. The game went 10 innings before St. Patrick's pulled out a 7-to-5 win.

However, in the days that followed people weren't talking about the fact that St. Michael's pitcher Dickle struck out 14 batters and allowed only six hits. No, they only wanted to talk about a single pitch that spun off the batter's bat and into the spectators. Eighteen-year-old William Callin was watching the game from about 50 feet behind the batter when the foul ball hit him in the neck.

While it most certainly hurt, the *Cumberland Evening Times* reported that "The injury was regarded trivial at the time but a serious condition developed within 48 hours." Callin developed neck pain where he had been struck watching the game at Johnson Farm on National Highway about two miles west of Frostburg. He died early in the morning on July 13. It was determined that the foul ball had fractured one of his vertebrae.

The young mine electrician for Brophy Mine was survived by both of his parents and four sisters. He was buried in Allegany Cemetery two days later.

You might think that death by baseball is an unusual way to die, but on the day that Callin was buried, the Midland and Moscow teams played a baseball game in Midland. A foul ball landed off the field near the crowd.

Thomas Johnson of Gilmore picked up the ball and threw it back onto the field, but not before it hit Cecil Thomas of Moscow. Thomas was the 17-year-old first baseman for the Moscow team.

"Johnson says he threw the foul ball back on the diamond in the direction of no one in particular and Thomas in attempting to catch it stumbled and fell, the ball striking him behind the left ear," the *Cumberland Evening Times* reported.

The blow from the baseball knocked Thomas unconscious and he died 10 minutes later without ever regaining consciousness from "a concussion of the brain."

A horrified Johnson turned himself in to the police. He was taken to Cumberland and held there overnight. State's Attorney William A. Huster, County Investigator Terrence A. Boyle and the county coroner meanwhile traveled to Midland to investigate the crime scene and question witnesses. The reason for the formal investigation was that it had been reported that there had been bad feelings between Thomas and Johnson.

As could be expected, the investigation confirmed Johnson's version of the story. He was released the day after the game when the investigators ruled that that the death had been an unfortunate accident.

Thomas, who was survived by his parents and a brother and sister was buried in the Laurel Hill Cemetery.

*This article originally appeared in the Cumberland Times-News on October 3, 2011.*

# Playing a game of "ride" and seek

Lester Albright, Leonard Bowling and Wilson Shulte scattered as one of their friends covered his eyes and began counting. They scurried around, searching for a place to hide; someplace they wouldn't be found. Crossing into the freight yards for the Western Maryland Railroad in Gettysburg, Pa., the boys climbed into a box car Friday morning, November 21, 1929.

Their hiding spot worked better than expected because they weren't found until Sunday afternoon. As the boys hid quietly in the box car, a trainman walked by making one last inspection of the train cars. Seeing the open box car, he shut the door and locked it.

Surprised, it took the boys a few moments before they realized they had been locked inside. When they did, they jumped from their hiding places and began banging on the door trying to attract attention. Then the train began moving!

Thus began their 118-mile journey to Cumberland.

Fighting down their initial panic, the boys thought it would be an adventure to take a short ride on the train, but then minutes turned into hours and the hours into days. The train did make one stop in Highfield, Pa., so that the train could be shifted to the main line of the Western Maryland Railroad.

The Western Maryland Railway began as the Baltimore, Carroll and Frederick Rail Road in 1852. It started in Baltimore and was built westward, eventually reaching Hagerstown, Md., in 1872. Within the next year after its founding, the company became the Western Maryland Rail Road Company and then later still, the Western Maryland Railway Company.

The company built an extension into Pennsylvania in 1881 and connected to the Harrisburg and Potomac Rail Road in 1886. Next, the Western Maryland Rail Road connected to the Baltimore and Ohio Railroad at Cherry Run, W. Va., in 1892. This connection improved freight traffic on the railroad.

An extension that ran to Cumberland was completed in 1906. From there, the railroad would extend to Connellsville, Pa., and south into West Virginia.

As passenger service declined in the 1950's, the Western Maryland discontinued it altogether in 1959. By 1973, the Western Maryland Railway became part of the Chessie System, which in turn became CSX Transportation in 1987.

"The first gnawing of hunger over-took the lads Friday evening. It was too cold in the car to sleep either night, and the boys kept awake by moving around," reported the *Gettysburg Star and Sentinel* on November 29, 1929.

On Sunday morning, a surprised trainman unlocked and opened the box car in the Western Maryland train yards in Ridgeley, WVa. The boys jumped out and asked how to get back to Gettysburg. The trainman turned the boys over to a railroad detective named Hanson. He listed to their story and turned them over to the Salvation Army in Cumberland and notified a local detective named Charles Wilson.

"After eating some hot food and a sleep, the trio were none the worse for their experience," the *Star and Sentinel* reported.

Wilson notified the boys' parents and Levi Albright and John Bowling, fathers of two of the boys, drove to Cumberland to pick up the boys on Sunday afternoon and drive them home.

The families had notified the Pennsylvania State Police when their sons hadn't returned home from playing on Friday, but the police hadn't been able to find any hint as to the boys' whereabouts.

*This article originally appeared in the Cumberland Times-News on November 9, 2009.*

# Of mice and women

It was the story of a little mouse named Mr. Mogo Mouse in . Czechoslovakia. As far as literature goes, it wasn't much of a story. What is remembered about *Mr. Mogo Mouse* 80 years after the book was published is the artwork.

The pages were filled with art deco illustrations, which one bookseller has said is similar to the work of *The Bobsey Twins* illustrator Janet Laura Scott. However, these illustrations were drawn by Jane Beachy Miller of Cumberland who was described as a pretty and "somewhat madcap" young artist by the *Cumberland Evening Times*.

Miller graduated from Allegany High and from there went on to the Maryland Institute of Art to pursue her passion as an artist. She graduated with an art degree and a scholarship that allowed her to travel through Europe in 1928 and study art.

Miller had always wanted to be an artist even as a young girl. "Even in her grammar school days, the local girl was more interested in art than in music which her mother was anxious for her to study," the *Cumberland Evening Times* reported. Her mother actually thought Miller's study of art was a waste of time and energy.

Even in art school, Miller challenged herself to expand her skills. She developed a children's series and began submitting her story and artwork to publishers.

"Why I even told her when she submitted her illustrated stories to the publishers, not to expect anything favorable as thousands of others are sending in the same kind of material week after week," her mother,

Mrs. Walter C. Ort, told the newspaper.

One publisher saw something in Miller's work, though. Publishing company P.F. Volland offered Miller a contract for what it said would be a new style of children's series written and illustrated by Miller. The first two titles in the series were called *Mr. Mogo Mouse* and *Trinkelette*. The expected publication date was 1929 or 1930.

The cover of Mr. Mogo Mouse a book written by Allegany High School Jane Beachy Miller before she was married.

Volland was a good place for a children's author to launch her career. P.F. Volland Company was founded originally as a greeting card company, but it quickly evolved into a book publisher with illustrators that included "Johnny Gruelle, Tony Sarg, Holling C. Holling, M.T. Ross, John Rae (of Howard Pyle's Brandywine School), John Gee, and

Maginel Wright Enright, the sister of architect Frank Lloyd Wright," according to the company's web site. P.F. Volland Company is probably best known as the publisher of the Raggedy Ann stories by Johnny Gruelle.

By the time word came out that Miller's manuscripts had been accepted, Miller was already on her way to Europe.

When the newspaper asked Miller's associates what they thought about her becoming a published author, it came as "complete surprise to her many friends who did not even suspect that she was adventuring in the field of literature," the *Cumberland Evening Times* reported.

*Mr. Mogo Mouse* was published in 1930 under the name Jane Ort (her stepfather was Walter C. Ort). It shows the signs of being a Depression-era book. After the stock market crash of 1929, P.F. Volland Company started using cheaper paper and covers to keep their costs low so the company could stay afloat. However, the company stopped publishing books in 1934 and there is no record of *Trinklette* being published.

Miller, who was called "one of New York's hardest-working young fashion illustrators" by the *Cumberland Evening Times*, went on to have a successful artistic career illustrating articles for magazines like *Good Housekeeping* and *Ladies Home Journal* with her pen-and-ink drawings. She also won an 1934 Art Directors Club Gold Medal beating out thousands of artists nationwide. Some of her drawings were included in Allegany County's Sesquicentennial Celebration in 1938.

*This article originally appeared in the Cumberland Times-News on October 31, 2010.*

# Einstein's secret vacation at Deep Creek Lake

Many people consider Albert Einstein the smartest man who ever lived. Yet, when this man who knew almost everything needed to unwind on summer, the vacation spot he chose was Deep Creek Lake.

Einstein vacationed for two weeks in September 1946 at the lake. He was seeking a place where he could find escape from the unwanted media that wrote about how his theories had led to the creation of the atomic bomb.

John Steiding of Midland invited Einstein to take a vacation at the lake. Steiding was a chemist at the Celanese plant and came to know Einstein through a co-worker's wife, who was sculpting the great man's bust. "Einstein, who wasn't very tall, found it uncomfortable to pose for the artwork since his feet would not touch the floor. John Steiding, being a handyman, made a footstool for Einstein," according to Francis Tam in an article called "Einstein in Western Maryland."

Besides being able to relax out of the national spotlight for awhile, Einstein was also able to have Dr. Frank Wilson examine him for an aneurysm of the aorta of the abdomen.

Einstein stayed at Wilson's lake cottage, the Mar-Jo-Lodge, for two weeks. "He took daily walks along the lake, frequently stopping to chat with strangers who had no idea who he was. He was sometimes seen fishing and also bird-watching with binoculars. He never skipped a meal but was a light eater. He drank a lot of water and lemonade; his favorite vegetable was fresh corn-on-the-cob from Garrett County," Tam wrote.

**Robbie Steiding sits on the lap of Albert Einstein during a 1946 visit that Einstein made to Western Maryland. The famous scientist was invited by Robbie's father, John Steiding of Midland, to vacation at Deep Creek Lake. Photo courtesy of Steve James.**

In particular, Einstein loved sailing, either with friends of alone. "During one of his many hours spent on the lake with Steiding, Dr. Einstein remarked that 'here you can get nearer to God,'" reported the *Cumberland News*. At times, "people would realize that he wasn't around, go searching for him, and find him in Harry Muma's little sailboat, 'single-handing,' on the Turkey Neck inlet," according to the Garrett County Historical Society's book, *Deep Creek Lake, Past and Present.*

During a visit, John Steiding's brother, Fred, asked Einstein asked to explain his famous theory of relativity in layman's terms.

"'Put it this way,' said Einstein, 'if you sit on a park bench with your sweetheart, an hour seems like a minute. If you sit on a hot stove by mistake, a minute seems like an hour,'" Tam wrote.

Einstein later said that his vacation at Deep Creek Lake was "one of the most restful and zestful vacations."

When the vacation ended, Einstein showed himself to be a generous guest giving Blair Thompson, who had attended him during the vacation, a $50 gratuity, which would equate to more than $1,000 today.

Following the vacation, he was back to work. In October, he wrote the United Nations said the organization should form a world government that maintained peace under the threat of nuclear devastation, according to Ze'ev Rosenkranz in *The Einstein Scrapbook.* Einstein also published his papers on his unified field theory in the 1950's.

To the world, the vacation remained a secret until the *Cumberland News* revealed the story in 1979.

*This article originally appeared in the Cumberland Times-News on November 7, 2008.*

# Santa and his city elves

While there may be old timers around who recall a time when Cumberland didn't welcome Christmas and feelings of "Peace of Earth Good Will to Men" that it brings, most of us know that the holiday season is upon us when Baltimore Street and the downtown Christmas tree light up.

Though the city's Christmas tree has not always been at the Isiminger Town Center, the City of Cumberland has had a Christmas tree for more than 63 years.

According to Diane Johnson, director of Cumberland's Parks and Recreation Department, the first record her department has of the city tree lighting is in 1947 and the first program they have is for the 1948 tree lighting. However, the city's sponsorship of a tree-lighting program dates back before World War II.

"Cumberland's first Christmas tree since the war will be lighted by Mayor Thomas S. Post during the hour-long community carol sing at 8 o'clock tonight in the City Plaza," reported the *Cumberland Evening Times* on December 16, 1947.

The post-war ceremony was another move towards normalcy after the restrictions and disruptions that residents experienced during the war years. More than 1,000 people turned out for the ceremony. Besides the community singing, the bands from Allegany High School and Fort Hill High School, the Fort Hill Mixed Chorus, the Allegany High Girl's Choir and the Cumberland Choral Society also performed

96

for the crowd.

Since that 1947 ceremony, the tree lighting has been an annual event. The following year, the ceremony moved to Riverside Park. In 1954, the tree lighting moved across Greene Street and up the hill to Emmanuel Episcopal Church. The most-recent move was in 1982 when the event moved to its present downtown location.

Location is not the only thing that has changed with the ceremony over the years. It has grown shorter and been moved to earlier in the season.

"Having a shorter ceremony gives people a more time to go the open houses and other activities," Johnson said.

For Johnson, her most-memorable tree-lighting ceremonies were the ones where Nicole Clulee-Cutter sang.

"She has such a beautiful voice," Johnson said. "When she sang 'O Holy Night,' you could hear a pin drop."

Though the city government no longer sponsors the ceremony, according to Johnson, it still helps out with personnel and other help. City personnel select the tree, cut it down, set it up in town, decorate it, decorate the downtown, participate in the tree-lighting ceremony and print up the program.

## Finding the perfect tree

The centerpiece of the city's tree-lighting ceremony is the Christmas tree so finding the perfect tree each year is important. This year's tree is a 35-foot-tall blue spruce that came from the First Christian Church, Disciples of Christ on Bedford Street.

When it comes to finding the just the right tree, the city turns to Marvin Myers and his expertise. Myers who recently retired from the Cumberland Parks and Recreation Department was asked to help the city find its tree this year.

"We start looking in October," Myers said. "People generally call in and we take their name and address and go look at the tree."

Myers said he seeks spruce trees that are 35 to 45 feet tall and close to the street so that the street department can get easy access to it. The tree also has to be relatively close to the city. Myers said the furthest he has ever had to go for a tree is Sunset Drive in Lavale or out on Oldtown Road. He looked at at least 18 trees this year to find Cumberland's perfect Christmas tree.

Myers said that most people who are willing to donate their spruce trees simply want to get rid of them because their size is causing problems on their property.

"It saves them $300 to $400 because they don't have to pay to have it cut down and they get credit at the ceremony," Myers said.

Once the street department personnel bring set the tree up in Downtown Cumberland, the decorating begins and takes about two days, according to Myers. Then the lights are switched on during the tree-lighting ceremony.

The 1948 Cumberland Christmas tree "which spectators last night termed the most beautiful they have seen, is illuminated not only by hundreds of colored lights but highlighted from beneath by a circle of green, neon lights," reported the *Cumberland Evening Times.*

Myers said he gets a "pretty good feeling" when the switch is flipped during the ceremony and all of the holiday lights come on. He said there was only one year when the lights didn't come on when the switch was thrown.

"We squirmed around under the tree for about five minutes until someone realized the automatic timer hadn't been turned off," Myers said. "It probably took about 10 minutes to get everything fixed."

## Here comes Santa Claus

One Christmas mainstay wasn't part of the early tree-lighting ceremonies, but Santa Claus is very popular part of the ceremony now. While the tree-lighting event takes less than a half hour, Santa remains for at least another hour and a half talking with children about their Christmas wishes.

Santa makes his entrance during the tree-lighting ceremony. He has entered downtown on trains, cars and carriages.

"The best entrance he has made is when he comes in a fire truck on the hook and latter in the bucket with the spotlight on him," Johnson said. He also comes with an entourage of elves, Rudolph the Red-Nosed Reindeer, Frosty the Snowman, police cars and more.

Since 1995, Santa Claus has also been known as Mike Nicholson.

"He has his own suit and he really takes it seriously," Johnson said. When he's not busy with his Santa duties, Nicholson works at the city's parks and recreation department.

"I love being Santa. I really do. I think I get more of a kick out of it than the kids do," Nicholson said.

Playing Santa Claus also fills a void for Nicholson.

"I was never blessed to have children so I call all of them my kids at Christmas," Nicholson said.

He said that listening to children's Christmas wishes can sometimes be a tough job because he has to keep himself from crying.

"Last year, a child told me she wanted her dad to come home from the war," Nicholson said. "I had to pause. I just let God fill my mouth with something to say."

However, what he says the most this time of year is, "Ho, ho, ho! Merry Christmas!"

*This article originally appeared in the December 2011/January 2012 issue of Allegany Magazine.*

# Saving Shallmar

As principal of the elementary school in Shallmar, Md., J. Paul Andrick knew all of his 50 students on a personal level. In a three-room school, that wasn't too hard to do. What was hard to do was watching those students literally fade away.

Shallmar was a small coal-mining town along the Upper Potomac River in Garrett County. It was a town on the edge of life and a short life it had been. Coal mining was the town's only industry. The Shallmar Mining Company had started large-scale mining in 1917 and the Wolf Den Mining Company took over operations in 1929.

During the peak-demand years of two world wars, 90 miners worked in the mine. Now only 53 miners lived in the company town and they hadn't worked full-time for years. In 1948, the Wolf Den Coal Company mine had operated for three months and before the mine had closed down at the end of March 1949, it had operated only 19 days that year.

The miners weren't giving up on the town, though. One unidentified miner told an Associated Press reporter, "I was born just up the river and I guess I'll die here."

His words came close to being prophetic for the entire town of 230 people.

Since school had reopened in September 1949, Andrick had watched his students lose weight and become listless. Some simply stopped coming to class. When one young girl fainted from hunger in mid-December, Andrick's eyes were finally opened to what was happening in the town.

He sent the girl home and when he checked up on her later, Andrick discovered that the family "had literally lived on apples for two weeks," he told a reporter for the Associated Press. Other families in Shallmar were just as bad off. "At another home a mother of seven told of feeding her family on bread, potatoes and beans for a similar period, then added, 'today for a change we had cabbage for supper,'" reported the Associated Press.

Nearly all of the 53 families in the small coal-mining town were starving. The company store had extended credit to the families after the mine closed in March, but the families were all maxed out by the fall. Not only that, but unemployment benefits to the miners had run out at the end of the summer. Some miners had tried to find work at other mines, but there was little work to be had. While other towns still had working mines or other industries, they could see their futures in Shallmar's present.

Shallmar was a planned mining town built by W. A. Marshall in 1917. Photo courtesy of the Garrett County Historical Society.

"Without a great amount of help from the outside, these people cannot hope to survive the winter," Andrick said.

When hunting season came in the fall, the miners had taken their rifles into the woods and brought four deer back to the town to be shared among the town. It wasn't a great bounty, but to those families with nothing, it was a feast.

One resident said, "I never cared much for venison, but it was the first fresh meat in this house in three months."

Andrick called the press's attention to Shallmar's woes and within days the story had been published in newspapers all over the world. The story touched people's hearts, particularly because it was less than two weeks before Christmas. Readers began to take action.

**The Children at Shallmar School had so little to eat in the fall of 1949 that as Christmas neared some of them were sick and fainting in class. Courtesy of Shirley Watts.**

## Christmas 1949 brighter in Shallmar

The town of Shallmar, along the Upper Potomac River in Garrett County, was dying. The Coal miners hadn't worked regularly for years and the Wolf Den Coal Corporation, the town's only industry, had shut down at the end of March 1949. By December, the town's 230 residents were starving until principal J. Paul Andrick called the world's attention to the town's plight.

On Dec. 12, two trucks rolled into Shallmar and were unloaded at the school. Then Andrick and Albert Males, chairman of the United Mine Workers local relief committee supervised the distribution of milk, eggs, fruits, vegetables and clothing to grateful residents.

"Christmas has come early to this destitute coal mine town. There were hot lunches today for the 50 pupils at the elementary school," the *Frederick News* reported.

**Other than the mining company in Shallmar, the company store was the only other business in Shallmar, though it was also owned by the mining company. The building was built by Italian stonemasons and is still standing today. Photo courtesy of the Albert and Angela Feldstein Collection.**

Shipments continued to come in. The closest communities – Cumberland, Frostburg, Midland, Westernport and Piedmont – sent help first. In Cumberland, the Lions and Optimists clubs set up a collection station and planned to send a daily truck to Shallmar. High school students in Cumberland held their own collection drives to raise money and collect donations.

After that first shipment, "Andrick estimated there is enough on hand so the gaunt coal miners and their families will have square meals for two or three weeks," according to the *Frederick News*.

To feed the 50 school children through June would require about $1,500 just for the food, which Andrick was hopeful could be raised to continue the hot lunch program for the children.

The trucks continued to roll into town coming from further and further away. In Baltimore, the American Legion made a call for donations and met with a strong response.

State Adjutant Daniel H. Burkhart said, "If I couldn't see it with my own eyes I wouldn't believe such a response was possible in three days."

Among the donations of food, clothing and cash, people also contributed fur coats and a baby carriage.

A grateful town received it all. "Stubble-faced miners, laughing women and kids with runny noses pawed over heaps of donated clothing today, picking out what fitted and hurried home to try it on. Many of the youngsters, however, couldn't wait. They just piled sweaters and coats over their summer-weight clothing on the spot," reported the *Hagerstown Morning Herald* on Dec. 14.

Also, when each family left the school, they left with a box full of food.

A picture of two-year-old Jean Ann Crosco, upset because she couldn't find shoes that fit her in the distribution pile, ran around the world. Within a month, Jean Ann had 100 pairs of shoes and cash donations made specifically to her.

"The flood of toys, candy, clothing, and money put new life into our town. I know the children are living in a different world since Santa made an unexpected appearance," Andrick said.

A month later packages were still coming into the small town. Andrick and four other people in town had formed a committee to manage the distribution of the donations and answer all of the mail. A total of $5,731 had been raised. Even more promising was that nine of the 50 miners in town had managed to find work elsewhere.

Shallmar's struggle had also given others aid. The *Cumberland Evening Times* reported, "Shallmar's plight also focused attention on a bad unemployment situation in the Cumberland area. Thousands of unemployed in Baltimore had also run through their jobless benefits.

"So the Maryland legislatures met in a special one-day session in December and appropriated $300,000 to help out such people 'unemployed employables'," reported the newspaper.

It had turned out to be a Merry Christmas after all.

*This article originally appeared in the Cumberland Times-News on December 27 and 28, 2007.*

*AUTHOR'S NOTE: You can read the full story about the Shallmar Miracle in my book, Saving Shallmar: Christmas in a Coal Town.*

# Tracking the underground Pony Express

Herds of ponies once roamed Maryland, though they were rarely seen my most people. They were mining ponies whose job it was to haul the coal from Maryland's coal mines.

In one instance, Ray O'Rourke wrote for the *Baltimore Sunday Sun Magazine*, "Twenty-odd ponies that haul coal from under some 2,000 acres of Maryland territory are never seen in this State, and never breathe the air over it."

These ponies hauled coal for the Stanley Coal Company in Crellin, Md. Though the mine was under Maryland, the entrance was in nearby West Virginia. Miners had to walk from Crellin across the state line and then backtrack once they were in the mine.

The mine's location also created some political headaches with Maryland and West Virginia governments fighting for the tax revenue from the mine. Eventually a compromise was reached where West Virginia inspected the mine while the miners paid Maryland income taxes and the Stanley Coal Company paid unemployment taxes to Maryland.

The ponies were stabled near the mine entrance in West Virginia so that is where Okey Jenkins, the stable boss, lived. At any given time, he had about 20 ponies that he cared for. Jenkins was a large man weighing in at 305 pounds at age 63. Besides stable boss, he also functioned as the harness maker, veterinarian, pony trader and pony trainer

106

for the mining company.

He worked out of a small 2-foot by 4-foot office with a sturdy swivel chair as its only furnishing. Harnesses, tools and surgical instruments hung from hooks on the wall.

Mining ponies and mules pulled coal cars for the coal companies in Western Maryland. They lived most of their lives underground. Courtesy of the Albert and Angela Feldstein collection.

Jenkins lived close by in a small house that showed his affection for horses. A merry-go-round pony was mounted on its pole in his front yard and pony bells served as his doorbell.

He left for work each morning at 4 a.m., walking down the hill to his small office. By 5 a.m., he was at work feeding all of the ponies and by 6:40 a.m., he would be harnessing the ponies and leading them to the mine where they would haul coal cars from 7 a.m. to 2:30 p.m.

"Unlike ponies that are kept underground all their lives in deep-pit mines, the Crellin ponies never contract the blindness that constant darkness brings," O'Rourke wrote.

Despite keeping their sight, the ponies still worked more than 400 feet underground. Ponies were used because they could work in low, narrow spaces. This meant that the mine shafts didn't need to be as wide as they have needed to be if small engines had been used to move the coal out of the mine.

The ponies worked hard in the mines. A 550-pound pony could pull a 2,200-pound coal car loaded with two tons of coal. Jenkins preferred ponies for this work because they didn't have to duck in the low-ceiling shafts as horses would have to do and their shorter height gave them a better angle to lean forward and pull the load. He was also partial to Welsh ponies for the work because he said they had greater stamina.

The ponies needed stamina, too. Besides having to pull such heavy loads, they might pull up to 50 such loads a day, though most days it was less.

"They're like high-strung men. They feel their responsibility, and they show it," Jenkins said.

The ponies and Jenkins worked six days a week. When he was off on a buying trip for more ponies, an assistant would work his shift. However, Jenkins always made sure to check on the ponies when he returned.

"Should any of them ever show welts or whip mark, he says: 'Better watch-there's gonna be a fit throwed around here. We don't want these little fellas all boogered up,'" O'Rourke wrote.

Part of this care came because Jenkins truly loved his ponies, but he was also protecting the mine's investment. Jenkins could buy an untrained pony for $250, but once it was trained, it was worth $1000. Keeping the ponies healthy also ensured many productive work years. A pony could start hauling coal at age three and continue until it was 25 years old.

*This article originally appeared in the Cumberland Times-News on March 8, 2010.*

# The boy who was missing part of his heart

James "Jim Boy" McKenzie of Lonaconing had lived nearly four years with only three-quarters of his heart, but time was running out for the young boy.

When Jim Boy was born in 1946, it was without the right ventricle of his heart. The right ventricle is one of the four chambers of the heart. It pumps deoxygenated blood from the heart through the lungs and back to the left atrium in the heart.

Without the ventricle, Jim Boy was able to live but he suffered from a unique version of the Blue Baby Syndrome. Blue babies have poorly oxygenated blood that is blue in color rather than red and this blue blood causes their bodies to look blue. In Jim Boy's case, it was only his hands, feet and lips that apparently turned blue.

His parents had taken Jim Boy to Johns Hopkins Hospital four times over his short life and "specialists informed them they could do nothing for Jim Boy at the time, but possibly could aid him if he lived a little longer," the *Sunday Cumberland Times* reported in December 1949.

So Jim Boy returned home with no relief in sight and his condition grew worse. He suffered an attack in August 1949 and was admitted to Allegany Hospital. For six weeks, Dr. Thomas Robinson watched over Jim Boy trying to find an effective treatment. Nothing worked.

Jim Boy was admitted to Johns Hopkins on Oct. 27 for the fifth, and what many people expected to be the last, time.

Doctors told the McKenzie family that things didn't look good for the youngster. He had two blood clots in the main artery leading to his heart and two more were forming in the main artery to Jim Boy's brain.

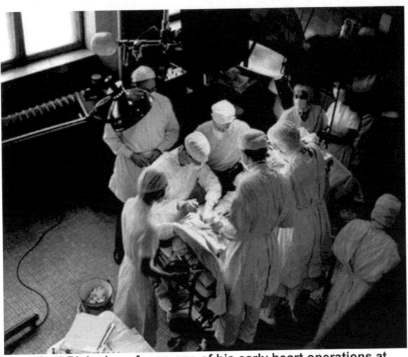

**Dr. Alfred Blalock performs one of his early heart operations at Johns Hopkins University. Courtesy of Alan Mason Chesney Medical Archives, Johns Hopkins University.**

Doctors Alfred Blalock and Helen Taussig took on the case and recommended surgery for Jim Boy, but they only placed his chances of survival at 60 percent. According to the *Sunday Cumberland Times*, "later the specialists gave him even lesser odds as he never ate much, weighed only 24 pounds, could hardly walk two feet without falling and his breath was very short."

Blalock was the surgeon-in-chief of Johns Hopkins Hospital and professor and director of the department of surgery of the medical school. He had become well known when he showed that shock generally came from the loss of blood. He recommended using plasma or whole-blood transfusions as treatment for shock, treatment that is credited with saving the lives of many casualties during World War II. He had also developed the technique to use shunts to bypass obstructions in the aorta.

Taussig's interest in cardiology and congenital heart disease led her to discover that the major problem with Blue Baby Syndrome was the lack of blood reaching the lungs to be oxygenated.

In 1943, she overheard a conversation Blalock was having with another doctor about his shunt technique when she began thinking it might have an application in treating Blue Baby Syndrome. She interrupted the conversation and began brainstorming ideas with Blalock.

From this conversation, Blalock and Taussig developed a successful way to treat Blue Baby Syndrome. The first operation using shunts to treat the defect took place in November 1944 and was successful. The following year, the pair published a joint paper on the first three operations in the *Journal of the American Medical Association.*

By the time Jim Boy came to them, Blalock and Taussig were famous for successfully treating Blue Baby Syndrome. If anyone could help Jim Boy, they could.

The surgery lasted four hours, during which they transferred the main artery of Jim Boy's right arm to his heart and a near-normal function returned to the boy's circulatory system, according to the *Sunday Cumberland Times.*

A half an hour after the operation, Jim Boy was conscious enough to recognize his mother and his lips were already turning pink.

By post-operative day two, he was more talkative and on day three the nurses were calling him "Chatterbox." He was released from the recovery room to a regular room on day four.

In the following month, Jim Boy gained two pounds, his chest expanded and he grew 1.25 inches.

His parents said, "The two doctors who have restored the warmth to our son's hands and feet certainly have put a warm spot for them in our hearts."

*Update to the story:* I heard from Joanne Spiker, Jim Boy's sister, after the article ran. She updated me on what her brother's life had been like. He had married, but he died young at age 54 in 1999. He had three children—Jim, Kim and Tim. Though Jim Boy was unable to work full-time, he still managed to do computer work from his home in York, Pa. Spiker said that one of the odd effects of her brother's medical condition was that he never had a pulse in his right arm. "He had to wear a necklace that alerted emergency personnel that if they didn't feel a pulse it didn't necessarily mean he was dead," Spiker said.

*This article originally appeared in the Cumberland Times-News on April 4, 2010.*

# First English Baptist Church warm with love

Outside, the day was blustery and cold on January 30, 1950, but inside the First English Baptist Church parsonage in Frostburg, it was warm with love. Rev. D. A. Vossler was marrying Thomas Brownfield and Ellen Jan Sprowl.

"During the hushed rites, which omitted the word 'obey,' Ellen Jane gazed calmly at the man who soon was to claim her as his own. Her black hair with its neat white ribbon capped a Navy blue silk dress with demure red trimming," The *Morning Herald* in Uniontown, Pa. reported about the wedding.

Brownfield himself was described as wearing a blue serge suit. Sarah Moats and Lois Balsinger, both of Haydentown, Pa. were both in attendance for the bride.

It was a typical picture of the commitment of love between two adults.

There was only one problem. The bride wasn't an adult. She was only 17 years old.

And the groom was 79 years old.

William A. Wilson, license clerk, checked the records at the Allegany County Court House and said the ages listed on the marriage license were 51 years old for Brownfield and 38 years old for Sprowl.

"Wilson said that he does not remember exactly if the man obtained the license alone but in no event was a girl who gave her age as 17 years granted a license," reported the *Cumberland Evening Times* on February 9, 1950.

Vossler said he had interviewed the couple and been told neither had been divorced. He had also interviewed the bride's attendants.

"I had no reason to doubt the facts as contained on the marriage license and married the couple in good faith," Vossler told the *Cumberland Evening Times.*

He did admit that Sprowl looked younger than 38, but certainly older than 17. The Morning Herald described Sprowl as a "wholesome belle of the fresh, green West Virginia ranges" with blue eyes and weighing 135 pounds.

Following the wedding, Brownfield said the love he had "sought so long" had finally come to him.

Sprowl was more practical in her reasons. She had lived in a log cabin until three months prior to her marriage and she longed for a "home of my own." She got it with Brownfield who had a nine-room farmhouse on a 60-acre farm in Fairchance, Pa.

No mention is made of what Sprowl's parents thought of the marriage, but the teenager was still married more than six months later when she became a widow.

According to the *Morning Herald,* Brownfield died of injuries from a fall from his sister's porch in Ronco, Pa. He and his young wife had been visiting Brownfield's sister, Hattie Frey, who was sick, and staying with her.

No mention was made of how Brownfield fell or whether there were any suspicious circumstances.

However, besides lying about their ages, it also appeared that the couple lied about whether Brownfield had been married before. The same newspaper that noted in February that Brownfield had never been married, wrote in August that he was survived by five children from a previous marriage, including one daughter, Dorothy Moat of Haydentown, who may have been related to one of Sprowl's bridemaids.

*This article originally appeared in the Cumberland Times-News on February 14, 2008.*

# Bittinger gets dial-up phone service

When the storm came through Bittinger in January 1953, no one could have imagined that the ice that fell would change the way of life in the small town in Garrett County.

*The Cumberland Evening Times* reported the storm's devastation, writing, "Then a sleet and wind storm struck in January 1953. It was one of the worst ever to hit the area and after it was over, the Bittinger Mutual Telephone Company was almost non-existent. Poles and wires were down and service paralyzed."

The Bittinger Mutual Telephone Company was a small cooperative that had kept the town's residents in contact with the outside world for 50 year. J.B. Emory, an 80 year old, blind, retired insurance agent, operated the switchboard from his house. He used a pre-World War I hand-operated switchboard and offered service from 7 a.m. to 10 p.m.

Bill Emory, J.B.'s grandson, lives is his grandfather's house in Bittinger. As a young boy, Emory remembers watching his grandfather operate the switchboard. "Everybody was on a party line. When a call came in, a little cover would fall down so you would know which line the call was on," Emory said.

Fern Beachy remembered that the phone system helped people in town keep up to date on what was happening. Each family had a particular type of ring made up a mixture of short and long rings. If your phone rang using someone else's series, you weren't supposed to answer it.

"But you knew another family was getting news," Beachy said. "If you wondered what was going on, you listened in."

Alice Orendorf lives in Bittinger. Her father-in-law Hugh Orendorf wrote his memories of the phone company in a memory book before he died. According to Orendorf, residents used to call J.B. Emory with their grocery orders. He would call them in to Harry Yommer in Grantsville, the town to the north of Bittinger. Yommer then made trips to Bittinger once a week to deliver the groceries.

Alice's mother-in-law Viola Orendorf recalls that residents also called in orders for cow feed that Emory would also take care of.

"He was blind so he couldn't write the orders down," Alice said. "So he had to remember them all and he did, too. No one every said they got the wrong order."

So when the ice storm crippled the phone lines, it crippled the town. *The Cumberland Evening Times* reported, "The sheer weight of the ice caused the poles to lean in grotesque angles. Ninety per cent of Bittinger Mutual's lines were down." This meant the 65 people in town didn't have phone service.

Nelson Orendorf, president of the phone company since 1936, surveyed the damaged after the storm, along with Vice President W.E. Buckel, I.O. Yaste and Marvin Bertzell. Repair costs added up quickly to an amount the cooperative couldn't afford. To do so would mean that cooperative would no longer be able to offer inexpensive phone service to its customers.

Negotiations began with C&P Telephone, which agreed to install the needed infrastructure to reconnect the community with the world. It was a hard decision, especially for Orendorf. The company had been around for 50 years and he had been its president for all but two of those years.

In May of 1954, ground was broken for new telephone poles. The new poles were installed every 35 feet instead of every 100-125 feet as Bittinger Mutual had done. This would give it better wind and sleet resistance. A new 15-foot by 17-foot building was constructed for the switching equipment. The repairs added up to $102,000 or about $750,000 in current dollars.

"The telephone company officials here prefer to believe that the

Bittinger job is the biggest little job it has undertaken in Maryland," the newspaper reported.

When the change to the dial-up service was complete, J.B. Emory was there to make one of the first calls on the new system. He dialed Milton Miller, the manager of the Springs Mutual Telephone Company in Grantsville.

"There was a touch of nostalgia as Emory informed Miller that he would no longer place calls to Grantsville from his switchboard but that all calls to Grantsville and Springs, Pa. would be routed through the new dial central office," *The Cumberland Evening Times* reported.

J.B. would die in 1958 so his grandson said his grandfather was not overly disappointed to lose his job. "He was getting up in years then," Bill Emory said. "It was time. I don't remember him having any hard feelings."

Grantsville's new exchange was "Chestnut 5", which still remains as the 245 prefix to Bittinger phone numbers.

*This article originally appeared in the Cumberland Times-News on April 30, 2007.*

# A picture's worth
# a thousand words

Thomas Connelly, a Times-News employee, stood next to a machine the size of a slot machine and took off the large strip of paper that it fed out. He studied the pictures on the page, gave his nod of approval and the *Cumberland Daily News* and *Cumberland Evening Times* became the first newspapers in Maryland to use the Photofax, a new process for transmitting pictures, in August 1955.

The first photograph had been transmitted electronically in 1922 over the telephone lines in Washington, D.C. By 1935, the Associated Press had adapted the technology to send pictures to its member newspapers so that they could be published.

The Associated Press was formed in 1848 as newspapers tried to cover a growing number of events with a limited number of reporters. AP was a cooperative organization between newspapers. One reporter could cover an event and share the article with member newspapers. So it was important for the reporter to be able to get the photographs from the event to the member newspapers in a timely manner.

Since telephone lines in the early part of the 20th Century were party lines, the AP used leased telephone lines on which only their photos could be transmitted. A single picture took minutes to send and in the days before e-mail, this was the fastest way to send images all over the world.

Electronic transmission of photographs gave birth to the "golden age" of photojournalism. Newspapers and magazines began attracting readers with the photographs they ran. Photographers like Robert Capa, Alfred Eisenstaedt, Margaret Bourke-White and W. Eugene Smith became well-known because their photographs appeared in a large number of magazines and newspapers. And the reason that could happen was because of electronic transmission of the photographs.

However, transmission using leased lines could only send the image to one newspaper at time, which made the process time-consuming. In 1952, a new machine was introduced that automated the process and made it even faster. The machine was called the Photofax.

The *Cumberland Evening Times* reported that by eliminating some of the operations required in leased-wire transmissions, the process would be simplified and bring "radical change in the reception of news pictures by wire."

Under the Photofax process, pictures were delivered for immediate use by a mechanical engraving process rather than the photo-electric process used by leased lines.

"Photofax is a facsimile process which receives news pictures on sensitized paper, instead of photographic film or photographic paper. The picture comes from the machine ready for the engraver and in a matter of minutes is ready for publication in a newspaper," reported the *Cumberland Evening Times*.

A Photofax could send a picture to 400 newspapers in seven minutes.

"Its installation in Cumberland means that every picture transmitted will be on hand for study and selection of the best to be used in the Times and News," reported the *Cumberland Evening Times*.

The first major test of Cumberland's Photofax system was to send out pictures from Cumberland's bicentennial celebration, which began the following day. Because the newspaper was able to send out photos to many other newspapers quickly, the celebration got a lot more national recognition than it might have otherwise.

*This article originally appeared in the Cumberland Times-News on April 14, 2008.*

# When Cumberland men were very hairy

Things got a bit hairy in Cumberland as its 200th birthday celebration neared. Normally clean-shaven men began to show permanent five o'clock shadows that grew darker as the summer grew hotter. They spurned the razor and worked at their jobs or attended church with a growing amount of hair covering their faces and chins.

They were the Brothers of the Brush.

As part of the celebration of Fort Cumberland's bicentennial, "Men were encouraged to grow beards or purchase a "permit" to shave. The publicity stunt attracted nation wide attention," according to *Primetime: A History of Allegany County During the 1950's.*

The Brothers of the Brush began in May 1955 when about 1,800 men scorned their razors and banded together into chapters with names like "Kasey Clippers" or "Down in the Valley."

The Cumberland Brothers of the Brush weren't the first group to grow beards in celebration of an important anniversary. For instance, Lawrence, Mass. celebrated its centennial in 1953 with the help of Brothers of the Brush and even as late as this year, Tulsa, Okla., celebrated its centennial with the Brothers. The term itself dates back to at least the mid-1700's.

Not to be left out of the spotlight, women formed the Bonnet Belles and began wearing bonnets around town.

As summer progressed and the elaborate plans for the celebration began to unfold, other signs of the bicentennial appeared. The *Cumberland Evening Times* reported that the Allegany County courthouse and Union Street buildings were "decked out with American flags and bunting at a cost of $215."

The newspaper also noted that, "It has been the source of much humor as residents watch the progress of the growth and the variety of the designs" of the beards appearing around town.

As part of the week-long bicentennial celebration, August 18 was designated Belle and Brush Day. The Bonnet Belles conducted a fashion show featuring fashions from the colonial period, the Gay 90's and the Roaring 20's.

However, the event of the day was judging of the beards at Fort Hill High School at 5:30 p.m. Winners were selected for best full beard, best goatee, best Irish beard, best mutton chops, blackest beard, most brown beard, reddest beard, whitest beard, longest beard, best two-toned beard, best sideburns and most pitiful beard. Edward Malloy took the award for overall award when the winners were announced at 8:15 p.m. All of the winners received electric shavers.

However the competition was not over yet. The *Cumberland Evening Times* called what followed, "The roughest event of the day – a shaving contest which followed the judging – was won by Oscar Peer, who removed a full beard by an electric shaver in seven minutes, winning by a few mustache hairs over Ray Baker."

The Fort Cumberland Bicentennial was not the end of the Brothers of the Brush in Allegany County.

They reappeared in the summer of 1962 for the Frostburg Sesquicentennial. Tom Robertson wrote in a 2002 *Frostburg Express* article about his memories of the event.

"It seemed as if most of the men of the town had lost their razors! Beards, goatees, mutton-chops adorned the chins and cheeks of many usually clean-shaven citizens. But it was not a wild rebelliousness or reverting back to a more primitive nature that brought about this change. No, what had happened was Sesquicentennial fever had come to Frostburg!" he wrote.

Frostburg's celebration ran from June 29 to July 7, 1962, and once again, the men of Allegany County formed into chapters of the Brothers of the Brush. This time the chapters had names like "Pie McGuire's

Brush Boozers", "Jiggiloes" and "Layman's Has Been Brothers", according to Robertson.

The Bonnet Belles also made their return in Frostburg, though this time they were called the Frosty Belles.

"Week- long activities from parades to pageants to pancake breakfasts were held in town. Men grew beards; women wore long dresses and bonnets. We were 'Victorians' and pioneers, Keystone Kops and Civil War soldiers ... the town was in the mood to celebrate and celebrate we did!" Robertson wrote.

The Brothers of the Brush have vanished since that time, but in 2012, Frostburg could celebrate its bicentennial and once again the men of the area might be called upon to join the brotherhood.

*This article originally appeared in the Cumberland Times-News on June 20, 2007.*

**Next page: The men of Cumberland formed the "Brothers of the Brush" by not shaving during the celebration of Cumberland's 200th birthday in 1955. From the Herman and Stacia Miller Collection courtesy of the Cumberland Mayor and City Council.**

# Life in the fast lane

While most kids were playing outside during the spring and summer of 1955, Roger Taylor of Wiley Ford spend untold hours indoors working. Even though he was a young teen, Roger was doing engineering and design on paper and then making his designs a reality.

He was building a racing car.

No, not a motorized automobile but an original "sleek, laminated-wooden racer which Junior Association of Commerce inspectors called the best-constructed coaster ever to run in eight years of Derby competition here," reported the *Cumberland Times* about Roger's soapbox derby racer.

"I came up with the design and my parents and neighbors helped me build it," Roger said in a recent interview.

Roger had built his own soapbox derby racer that he hoped would win him a national soapbox derby title, but first he had to win the Cumberland competition.

The race was held on July 16, 1955 on Pennsylvania Avenue. Taylor easily beat the field of about 50 competitors. Not only did Oscar Lashley present him the winning trophy but he received the Shell Oil Company's tool board for having the best-constructed car in the race. His chances at the national competition looked promising.

So on August 10, 1955, Roger and his parents flew out of the Blair County Airport in Martinsburg and headed for Akron, Ohio, to compete in the 18th Annual All-American Derby.

The competition was held on Aug. 15 and Roger would be facing

154 other local champs from the United States, Canada and West Germany. From Maryland, Baltimore, Hagerstown and Frederick also sent their champions.

Up for grabs was $15,000 in scholarships, including $5,000 (about $40,000 in today's dollars) for the grand champion.

"They had us on a tight schedule," Roger recalls. "We were busy from time we got there."

Then came race day and Roger's first race. Forty to 50,000 people were in attendance. The day was cold and overcast. A light drizzle occurred on and off.

Soapbox racing wasn't without its dangers in those conditions. Thomas Rappe of Decatur, Ill. lost control in the 41st heat, hit a sideboard and overturned. He was carried out of the race in a stretcher.

In Roger's heat, his racer took off and at one point was three lengths ahead of the next closest competitor. But then his lead began to shrink as his windbreak actually began to slow him down. At the 800-foot mark he was only leading slightly.

"The faster I went I could tell that I had a wind problem. Race Street didn't run that fast so it hadn't been a problem in Cumberland," Roger said.

Then the race ended and no one was quite sure who won.

"I didn't know at first I had lost. It took a minute and half to see the photo finish" Roger said.

Though leading for most of the race, he lost by six inches.

The winner was David Leroy O'Donnel of Deluth, Minn. who finished the day in the top 10.

However, Roger didn't go home empty handed. He got the best brakes award for a design of his own. His award was the first official award Cumberland had received in eight years of competing in the national soapbox derby.

"Several B.F. Goodrich inspectors called Taylor's brakes the most efficient they had ever seen in the 18-year history of the All-American," the *Cumberland Times* reported. "Linkage for the 1955 All-American's best brakes was dreamed up in just about every room in the Taylor home in Wiley Ford. This linkage is made from plywood and Roger ruined two pairs of his mother's best scissors cutting out cardboard which used as a pattern."

Taylor also got kissed by movie star Dinah Shore when he received his award.

"I wouldn't wash the side of my face for a month because Dinah Shore kissed me there," Roger said.

The 1955 grand champion was Dick Rohrer of Rochester, N.Y., a 14 year old who stood 6 foot 1 inch tall. He set a new speed record with the help of 20 mph winds 975.4 foot course. Following his win, the Goodyear blimp, which was flying overhead, broadcast the champ's name.

Nowadays, Roger doesn't catch the local soapbox derby because he's out of the town on that race day, but he still watches the national competition on television.

"I guess some of these kids now run their cars through wind tunnels. It takes a lot of labor to build a car, but it's well worth the effort to go to the nationals," Roger said.

*This article originally appeared in the Allegany Magazine June/July 2009 issue.*

# I now pronounce you husband and wife

"We are gathered here to join this man this woman together in matrimony. The contract of marriage is a most solemn one and not to be entered into lightly but thoughtfully and seriously and with deep realization of its obligations and responsibility. If anyone can show just cause why they should not be lawfully joined together let him speak now, or else forever hold his peace," Richard L. Davis said on January 2, 1964, as he performed the first civil marriage in Garrett County.

He stood in a room on the second floor of the Garrett County Courthouse, "decorated especially for the occasion and future civil marriages," according to *The Oakland Republican*.

A 1963 act passed by the Maryland General Assembly made it legal for clerks of the circuit court to perform civil marriages. The change took effect with the new year, but since New Year's Day was a legal holiday, the first civil marriages in Maryland couldn't happen until Jan. 2. Maryland was the last state in the country to allow civil marriages.

"Do you take this woman, Margaret Ann Durigon, to be your lawfully wedded wife?" Davis asked. He had to couple join hands. "Now repeat after me, I, Bernard Benjamin Bialon, take this woman, Margaret Ann Durigon, for my lawful wife to have and to hold, from this day forward, for better or for worse, for richer, for poorer, in sickness and in health, until death do us part."

Durigon was 20 years old and lived in Keisterville, Pa. She worked as a stripper for a textile mill. Bialon was 21 years old and lived in Uniontown, Pa. He worked as a machinist for the same mill.

The small ceremony had no witnesses, but none were required for Maryland marriages. It was just Davis and the couple.

"Place the ring on her finger and say, 'With this ring, I thee wed,'" Davis instructed Bialon.

**The Garrett County courthouse where couples could be married in civil ceremonies beginning in 1965. Photo courtesy of the Albert and Angela Feldstein Collection.**

It was almost accidental that Durigon and Bialon became the first couple wed in a civil ceremony in Garrett County. According to *The Republican*, another couple had wanted to be the first couple, but they didn't have the $10 cost for the service.

The cost for a civil ceremony at the time was $10 in addition to an application fee of $1 and a $4 marriage license. Durignon's and Bialon's cost $5 since they were county residents.

From the revenue generated by the license and application fees, $2 went to the county government. In turn, the Garrett County Commissioners turned over 85 percent of the amount to the Ruth Enlow Library and 15 percent to the Garrett County Historical Society. The remaining revenues from the fees stayed in the clerk's office.

Of the $10 cost for the civil ceremony, $8 went into the Garrett County general fund and $2 went to the clerk's office.

"By the power and authority vested in me as clerk of the Circuit court for Garrett County, Md., and I now pronounce you man and wife," Davis said, and so history was made and future created.

In the first eight days of 1964, 24 marriage licenses were applied for and seven of the couple requested civil ceremonies.

*This article originally appeared in the Cumberland Times-News on June 29, 2009.*

# Schools consolidate into Bishop Walsh

Fighting back tears, 80 young women formed an honor guard for the 18 graduating girls in the Class of 1966 from Catholic Girls Central High School on June 5. These were not so much tears of joy but tears for the end of an era. Catholic Girls Central, LaSalle High and Ursuline Academy were graduating their last classes and closing their doors.

In the fall, student would be attending Bishop Walsh High School. The *Cumberland Evening Times* reported, "This, the area's newest high school is said to be one of the most modern and complete educational plants in the state."

Catholic Girls Central commencement exercises followed a 12:15 p.m. Mass at St. Patrick's Church. The Rev. E. J. Herbert celebrated the Mass and delivered the commencement address.

Each of the girls was handed her diploma by Right Rev. Msgr. George Hopkins and the Rev. John Lyness.

Carol Madeline McKay of Frostburg won the award for the highest general average for her four years of high school.

Catholic Girls Central dated back to 1867 when the St. Edward Academy was opened by the Sisters of Mercy. the school offered a two-year secondary school course to girls. In 1888, the Sisters of St. Joseph from Ebensburg, Pa., replaced the Sisters of Mercy and allowed boys to enroll. In 1908, the School Sisters of Notre Dame replaced the

Sisters of St. Joseph. They extended the program to three years and changed the name to St. Patrick's High School, which offered both scientific and commercial courses. They also went back to being all girls. Three students graduated in 1908.

Catholic Girls Central opened in 1923 and increased the program to four years.

LaSalle's final commencement was held in the Allegany High auditorium on June 6, 1966. Hopkins also presented the awards to the graduates at this ceremony and Frank Florentine of Cumberland was the valedictorian. Diplomas were given to 71 graduates.

"My feeling was I would miss going to the new school because Brother James, who taught physics and chemistry, had designed the blueprints for the new labs in the school," said Tim Scaletta, who was a member of the last graduating class.

"I think a lot of the guys were a little reluctant to leave LaSalle. ... There were a lot of sad eyes when they closed their doors," said George Geatz, who was a sophomore during LaSalle's last year.

He remembers fondly the camaraderie of the school and things like "rookie week" when freshmen were assigned an upperclassman mentor or "initiation week" when freshmen were subjected to the wished of the upperclassmen in playful pranks.

LaSalle first opened its doors in 1907 at the corner of Smallwood and Fayette streets with 28 students. By 1909, enrollment had grown so much that a home on the opposite corner had to be purchased to accommodate the growing enrollment. It was originally called the LaSalle Institute and became LaSalle High School in 1938.

"From the time you could stand and walk, you dreamed about going to LaSalle. It was a natural progression for youngsters who went to St. Patrick's. LaSalle was just across the yard. You could go over there and see all the athletes they wrote about and all the guys you looked up to," said Scaletta.

Ursuline at S.S. Peter and Paul was established in 1892 under the pastorship of the Rev. Herman Peters. Ten students enrolled the first year and four students graduated in the first class of 1896. Linda Castle of Bowling Green was the valedictorian.

*This article originally appeared in the Cumberland Times-News on June 29, 2009.*

# Remembering the Hyndman flood

The heavy rains began Saturday August 11, 1984, and continued through the weekend. With that much water hitting the ground, it had to go somewhere. It ran into Wills Creek until the creek bed could no longer hold the water.

Then the flooding began sending six feet of water through Hyndman causing 85 percent of the population of Hyndman and Glencoe to be evacuated.

"You have to be a native of here to appreciate the weather in the Alleghenies. It can change and befuddle you in the shake of a hand," Hyndman Mayor Tom Cunningham told the *Daily Intelligencer*.

## The flood

Joy Carpenter worked at the bank in Hyndman in 1984. She and the other employees had just closed up for the day when they heard the sound of rushing water.

"We looked up the street and saw a wall of water heading toward us," Carpenter said.

The bank employees rushed to move stuff up onto the second floor. Then the back door to the bank burst open under the weight of the water pressing against it and 5.5 feet of surged into the bank.

"You think of floods as coming gradually," Carpenter said. "This one didn't and the water roared."

Carpenter and another woman sought safety on the countertops, which had been islands in the sea of roiling water in the bank. Caught inside the bank, the water level continued to rise.

"I thought I was going to die," Carpenter said.

She was making plans to take her chances in the debris-filled water when the front door to the bank broke open on some of the water rushed out seeking its own level.

Carpenter was lucky. Elsewhere in Hyndman, three men took shelter from the rain and flooding in a garage. The water rose quickly trapping the men inside the garage.

"One minute the building was there, the next minute it just seemed to pick itself up, fold together and wash downstream," resident Linda Applling told the *Indiana Gazette* on Aug. 15.

Clyde Burley of Bel Air, Md.; Robert Gibbner and Samuel Leydig, Jr., both of Hyndman, were drowned in the flood waters.

Pamela Phillipi was one of two Glencoe residents who died in the flood. The other was Charles Merkel who was sucked under the flood waters after he helped Phillipi's two children reach safety.

Pennsylvania State Police said that Merkel's 17-year-old son saw his father swept away in the flood.

Steve Leydig was working in Corriganville when he got a call from his worried wife at their home in Hyndman. He tried to get home to her, but the roads into Hyndman were impassable because of the flooding. He called his friend Tom Goetchius with Mattingly Construction in Cumberland, who got permission to use the company helicopter to help. Goetchius picked up Leydig and they flew into Hyndman. They began airlifting people stranded on roofs and in trees to the safety of the high school. They made seven trips, rescuing at least 25 people.

Besides the five deaths, a number of injuries were reported. Hilda Raupach, 84, of Glencoe was hospitalized in Somerset Community Hospital with chest pains. Her husband, Henry, also 84, was examined and released after he spend seven hours stranded in a tree.

## After the flood

On Tuesday, Aug. 13, volunteer workers joined the police to

search through the mud and debris that the receding flood waters left piled along Wills Creek.

"The landscape was littered with homes smashed against trees, swept off foundations or resting atop crushed cars. Trees and power lines lay along the creek and thick mud covered roads," reported the *Daily News*.

After walking through the devastated areas on Wednesday, Pennsylvania Governor Dick Thornburgh declared Bedford, Somerset, Allegheny, Armstrong, Blair and Westmoreland counties disaster areas.

"It's devastating, no question," Thornburgh said. "When you see the swath cut by a single body of water, it's unbelievable."

These counties had a combined total of around $4 million damage to state roads, highways and bridges. Thornburgh also ordered 40 Pennsylvania National Guardsmen to the area to help search for missing and help with the cleanup. The governor also authorized local officials to use their emergency powers to employ temporary workers, rent equipment and sign contracts without soliciting bids, according to the *Indiana Gazette*.

Hyndman Mayor Tom Cunningham estimated the damage in town at $10 million. More than 250 of the town's 420 homes were damaged. Forty families were given temporary shelter in Hyndman High School, where volunteers provided them with hot food and fresh water.

"This is the worst mess I've ever seen. We're going to be cleaning up here for a long time to come," said resident Ralph Kifer.

Even among the devastation residents refused to leave their homes. Even when more bad weather threatened, most residents stayed with their homes.

Volunteers turned out in the hundreds to help the community dig out.

"It's been unbelievably gratifying. People seem to have from all over this part of the state to help us, and from West Virginia and Maryland, too," Cunningham said.

## The search for bodies

Volunteer firefighters found Samuel Leydig's and Gibbner's bodies the morning after the flood. Merkel's body was found later that afternoon along Wills Creek about three-quarters of a mile from his where his two friends' bodies were found.

"I'm proud of him. I'm proud of both of them. They saved a lot of kids here. My son was with him 'til he went down and we're thankful that Chucky managed to come back," said widow Betty Merkel to the *Daily News*.

## The cleanup

Disaster relief checks began arriving three days after the flood when Ken Poland of Hyndman got the first check.

"I was surprised I got it so fast. Not only that, I thought I would only be eligible for a low-interest loan, but they gave me a grant," Poland told the *Daily News*.

Poland's basement and most of the first floor of his house flooded out. He lost two furnaces and had to have his electrical system replaced.

Bedford County had 323 applications for federal help. Somerset County had 93 and McKean County had 80 applications.

Some residents blamed the state for the flooding, saying they had asked for years for flood-prevention improvements and that the Pennsylvania Fish Commission had even stopped local efforts to dredge Wills Creek.

"The borough asked the (state) Department of Environmental Resources for help, but they said we didn't have enough flood damage in the area. I guess we have enough now," Baron Leap, Hyndman's public works foreman told the *Indiana Gazette*.

Pennsylvania officials responded saying that dredging wouldn't have lessened the damage.

*This article originally appeared in the Allegany Magazine August/September 2009 issue.*

# Creating ways west: Irish on the railroad and canal

On July 12, 2008, a Celtic cross was unveiled on the Crescent Lawn at Canal Place in Cumberland. It stood six feet tall and was made of Georgia granite. It also marked the completion of nearly 10 years of work by the Ancient Order of the Hibernians to see the cross erected.

The cross is not intended to be a religious symbol but a monument to the Irish laborers who died building the Chesapeake and Ohio Canal and the Baltimore and Ohio Railroad.

## Bringing the Irish to America

In the early 1800's as construction loomed for the C&O Canal and B&O Railroad, both companies sought workers in England, Scotland and Ireland. Company agents abroad placed ads in the city newspapers that promised workers three meals a day with meat, bread and vegetables. They also offered "a reasonable allowance of whiskey" to each worker. Pay was advertised at $8-$12 a month and $20 for masons.

Irish-American newspapers like the *Boston Pilot* attempted to warn the Irish immigrants about what they were getting in by running articles and editorials about how hard and dangerous the work was and that it was "the ruin of thousands of our people" who were treated like "slaves."

The problem was that unemployment in Ireland was high and so was the cost of living. Men seeking work knew they could find it in America and while it might be hard, at least they would be earning pay.

The workers were offered free passage to America in exchange for four months of indentured servitude.

"The truth was that they came at their own expense. In effect, the company advanced them the price of their passage, and got from each of them four months' hard, not to say cruel and unual, labor to pay back the cost," Elizabeth Kytle wrote in *Home on the Canal.*

Ships began sailing for America in August 1829. The canal workers debarked in Georgetown and Alexandria, Va., for fear that other employers might steal them away if they were brought to other ports.

"Some of the immigrants had refused to acknowledge indentures, and almost the first thing they saw in the new world was the inside of a jailhouse," Kytle wrote.

Others left when they became disillusioned with canal work and some of them did find other work.

The C&O Canal Company decided in October to drop the idea of indentured servants and instead raised the price of passage to America.

## Problems

The Canal Company also brought German workers to America. This created problems on both the canal and railroad. Because of the differing religions of the two groups, there was a lot of tension when the two had to work together. Fights broke out so often that the groups were kept separated.

Living conditions for the workers weren't the greatest either. Dysentery and tuberculosis were common. Accidents on the job were also frequent.

In August 1832, cholera hit the workers on the C&O Canal. The Irish working on the canal opposite of Harpers Ferry, W.Va., were the first victims as the disease swept through Washington County. Special cemeteries had to be created because residents were afraid to bring the bodies into populated areas. The workers themselves weren't any braver. They fled the canal when they realized what was happening.

"For most of them it was too late and they managed to get only 5 to 15 miles from the canal before death overtook them," Kytle wrote.

# Riots

When things got to be too much for the workers, they rioted. One large riot began on January 20, 1834, between Corkmen and Longfordmen. The fighting began when a Corkman killed John Irons, a Longfordman. Several people were killed in the first skirmish.

Local militia arrested 34 men and Williamsport residents tried to create a barrier between the two groups of Irish workers.

Fighting broke out again on Jan. 24. At least 600 Longfordmen attacked 300 Corkmen with guns, clubs and axe handles. More people were killed until the Corkmen fled. The Longfordmen chased them down.

The Washington County Sheriff William Fitzhugh brought two companies of militia to the area on Jan. 25 and forced the leaders to the come to terms and sign a peace treaty.

U.S. President Andrew Jackson sent two army units from Fort McHenry in Baltimore to patrol the canal and maintain the peace. This marked the first time the U.S. military were used in a labor dispute.

Other riots occurred between the Irish and German workers and Irish and Dutch workers over the years that canal and railroad were being built.

# Finding familiar work

The B&O reached Cumberland in 1842 and the C&O opened there in 1850. Once in Cumberland, many of the Irish workers decided to stay in the area because work was plentiful. Cumberland's immigrant population quickly grew.

"It is interesting that as Irish workers settled in Cumberland, they displaced the local Italians at the North End church," says Dan Whetzel, a local historian.

St. Mary's Catholic Church eventually changed its name in 1851 to St. Patrick's Catholic Church in recognition of the Irish congregation.

Many of the Irish workers found work in the coal mines of Allegany and Garrett counties. In 1850, Allegany County (which included present-day Garrett County) had 370 miners. The Irish made up the second-largest nationality group of the miners. There were 65 Irish miners who would help mine 240,000 tons of coal that year. By 1870, there were 2,463 miners in the Frostburg, Lonaconing and Westernport mining regions. Irishmen made up 369 of the miners.

## Irish monument

The Celtic cross monument at Canal Place cost $12,500 plus an additional $2,500 to establish a maintenance fund to care for the monument. The idea was first presented to the Canal Place Preservation and Development Authority in 2003. Members of the authority worried that the cross shape would cause a problem, but the Ancient Order of the Hibernians pointed out that it was the most-appropriate design for a monument that could be considered a grave marker for all the Irish workers who lost their lives building the canal and railroad.

*This article originally appeared in the Maryland Life March/April 2010 issue.*

# Whispers of communities gone

In the early years of the 20th Century, Kitzmiller, Maryland, was a boom town. With the discovery of coal in 1899, the town, nestled in a valley in Garrett County and alongside the Upper Potomac River, quickly grew. It had a bank, bakery, hotel, post office, high school, doctors, dentist, movie theater, barber shops, gas station and more. Just before the Great Depression the population was estimated at around 1,500 people.

Then the coal mines in the region began shutting down and people moved on to find work. Many of the businesses closed because their customers had gone. Today, the population is about 300 people.

Kitzmiller is actually quite lucky. It still exists even if it is a shadow of former self. The people who remain work hard to make it a good place to live, though they do so without many of the amenities the town used to have.

## Ghost towns

So many communities along the Upper Potomac are no longer. Some still have left behind a few houses or a road to nowhere that has fallen into disrepair, but even more have been totally swallowed up by the mountains.

Vindex, Md., had a company store that housed a post office and an open second floor that was used for recreational activities and theater productions. It had its own elementary school, though the high school students went to Kitzmiller. It also had 500 residents living in company-owned homes.

The children of Kempton, when the town was still a busy coal-mining town. It is now one of the ghost towns along the North Branch Potomac River. Photo courtesy of the Garrett County Historical Society.

Kempton, Md., began as a lumber town and continued life as a coal town. The company houses were built on a strip of land ¾ of a mile long and a few hundred feet wide. Each house had four or six rooms with a front yard and a garden in the back. Kempton had a school, an opera house and a company store that had a lunchroom, bowling alley, dance floor, auditorium and post office. A branch line of the Western Maryland Railway ran into the town.

Then the mines closed and, as happened with many of the company towns, the buildings were torn down to remove them from the tax rolls. In Kempton, thousands of dollars of company scrip were dumped down a mine shaft. The people moved on.

"They bought necessary commodities in company-owned stores and used company-issued scrip currency. They depended socially and economically on the success of their companies, and when their companies suffered, they suffered," Stephen Schlosnagle wrote in *Garrett County: A History of Maryland's Tableland*.

Vindex, Kempton, Shallmar, Wallman and others are gone with only a name and a few houses remaining to recall the memories of the towns that once thrived.

"Most of these ghost towns can be identified, when one finally reaches their locations, by ruins of old buildings amid the brush, cement foundations of former bridges, other structures, and remains of coal tipples. The real tombstones, however, are the large gob piles, partially hidden by tangled brush and scrub trees on the hillsides, that mark the coal mines that once gave life to so many of these old towns," George Fizer wrote in *Ghost Towns of the Upper Potomac*.

## When ghost towns thrived

The small coal and lumber towns along the Upper Potomac River were originally built to serve the needs of businesses in those remote areas. Houses were built for the employees. Because those employees were far from larger towns and cities (some could only be accessed by rail), businesses, schools, churches and post offices also needed to be built to provide for the needs of the employees. It was a symbiotic relationship between employee and business.

"When the timber and coal played out, the towns died—there was no longer a reason for their existence," says Dan Whetzel, a local historian with an interest in Western Maryland's mining region. "The rugged terrain and remoteness inhibited alternative reasons for the residents to remain there."

These small, isolated towns with populations anywhere from a couple hundred to 1,000 people tended to attract immigrants to work in the mines, mills and forests. The towns could be very homogenous, attracting mainly immigrants from a particular country.

"I suspect this was because families tended to draw other family members from abroad. Each town, therefore, had unique populations," says Whetzel.

However, when the mine or the mill shut down, the workers moved onto other small towns.

An old company house, in poor condition but still occupied. Photo courtesy of the Garrett County Historical Society.

# Union violence

On April 1, 1922, the United Mine Workers called a national strike. Many mines had low pay and poor working conditions, though miners in Western Maryland "were said to be generally satisfied with their wages and working conditions," according to Kathryn Harvey in *The Best-Dressed Miners*. However, she notes different companies were found to be underpaying their miners for the amount of coal they mined by using light scales.

The Knights of Labor, the American Miners' Association, Miners and Laborers' Protective and Benevolent Association and the United Mine Workers of America had all tried to unionize workers in the preceding years without much success. Garrett County miners walked out in support of the strike, which lasted until Aug. 15.

The mining companies, for their part, brought in strikebreakers from Ohio, Pennsylvania and West Virginia. Guards were armed with automatic weapons and even submachine guns.

The situation erupted in violence at various times. Dodson, Maryland, was one site along the Upper Potomac where miners and strikebreakers got into fights and fired shots at each other.

# Luke, Md.

Luke, Md., once had a 1,000 people living in it. Now with a population of around 73 people, it is one of the smallest municipalities in the state. The sole industry in the town is the MeadWestvaco paper mill, but the company has been struggling against foreign competition. This has lead to layoffs and furloughs. Others employees commute into town rather than live there.

Not that there are many places to live anymore. During the years when the plant was expanding, the company bought up properties to tear down the houses and grow.

The most-recent blow to Luke's livelihood is the closure of the U.S. Post Office at the end of April 2009. The reason given is that the U.S. Postal Service is struggling to remain profitable by reducing expenses. The Luke post office had generated only $100 in the last quarter of 2008 and the first quarter of 2009 and only four of the 60 post office boxes were rented.

Will Luke become another Maryland ghost town? That's for the future to decide. The remaining residents certainly hope not, but the town's population is smaller than most of the current ghost towns were at their peak and the town budget is nearly entirely dependent on taxes paid by MeadWestvaco.

*This article originally appeared in the Maryland Life July/August 2010 issue.*

# Making his list and checking it twice

According to Cumberland Postmaster Edwin Turner, citing studies completed by the U.S. Postal Service, half of people under 21 years old have never been to a post office.

"The volume is definitely not what it used to be," Turner said.

Even so, each year the Cumberland post office still gets around 80,000 pieces of mail between Thanksgiving and Christmas Day, according to Freda Sauter U.S.P.S. Corporate Communications Office.

While that is double the normal mail volume for that long a period of time, it pales in comparison to December 22, 1964, when the one-day total of mail cancellations through the Cumberland Post Office was 76,092 cancellations. The normal daily number of cancellations at that time was 15,000. During the Christmas period that year, the Cumberland Post Office cancelled nearly 1.3 million pieces of mail.

Many of those holiday cancellations are children's letters to Santa Claus.

One child's letter to Santa Claus, in 1911, which was published in the *Cumberland Evening Times*, read, "Dear Santa – Some people tell me there isn't any Santa, but you have been so good to me I know you must be real. I am not going to ask you for very much because I know you have so many boys and girls to visit that you cannot bring me everything I want, but I would like to have a rain cape, mother promised me one for my birthday, but she could not get my size in Cumberland, Md. perhaps you can get it in your land. I also want a sewing box, a little meat grinder, a roaster. I have a large doll, but I want a small one, which I can make dresses for myself, some storybooks, for I am very fond of reading, some games and candy, nuts and oranges. This is not all I want but I will not ask for anything else unless you have something to spare. Nellie Willison."

Cumberland and some other area post offices have a Santa box in their lobbies where children can mail their letters to Santa. From the post offices, the letters are sent to "Santa's elves" who read the letters and respond to the children's requests. Some of the elves are employees of the postal service while others are volunteers from the public.

"As close as we can tell, the Postal Service began receiving letters to Santa Claus more than 100 years ago," Sauter said. "However, it was in 1912 that Postmaster General Frank Hitchcock authorized local postmasters to allow postal employees and citizens to respond to the letters in the program that became known as Operation Santa."

As the popularity of the program and the volume of mail grew, the Postal Service became overwhelmed in trying to respond to all of the mail. To keep from disappointing children across the country, civic organizations, charitable groups and corporations were invited to become one of Santa's elves and help answer the mail. They not only wrote personalized responses, they also sent small gifts to the children who wrote to Santa.

"Letters to Santa are one of the department's big problems," the *Cumberland Sunday Times* reported in 1952. "If rules were followed strictly all of them would end up in the Dead Letter Office. But even the Post Office department has a conscience. It shuts its official eyes to allow individual postmasters to screen the Santa letters."

In the first half of the 20th Century, the Cumberland newspapers also helped make sure Santa knew what children wanted for Christmas. In 1929, Melvin McKenzie, Jr.'s letter to Santa showed what was on his mind: "Dear Santa, I am a little boy four and a half years old. I have tried to be a good boy so you could bring me a dump truck to help Daddy haul rock, a little saw, a pair of bedroom slippers and a little bus if you have room to put it in your sack; if not, all right. Don't forget to trim our tree and bring some candy, nuts and oranges. And please, Santa, don't forget sister."

The Operation Santa part of the Postal Service Christmas customer services involves the letters that come from adults – parents, friends, family – who write asking for help during the holiday season. Rather than toys, these letters ask for food, clothes, etc. to help a family get through a tough financial time. All of these letters, which are mailed in Maryland, are sent to the Baltimore Main Post Office.

"Individuals interested in adopting a letter will go in person to the post office, select the letter or letters and sign a form," Sauter said. "The Postal Service changed the letter adoption process in 2009 by mandating that the last name and address of the children writing to Santa be redacted so the individual adopting the letter could not see that information."

The redacted letters are now assigned a number that matches it to the correct name and address of the family.

"The postal clerk will match the number on the letter with the child's address, the customer will pay the postage, and the package will be mailed," Sauter said.

Besides being mailed and published, letters to Santa Claus have also played a role in the theater. The Beall High School Christmas assembly in 1960 included letters from students and faculty members being read to Santa by his elves as well as songs from the choir.

*This article originally appeared in the December 2011/January 2012 issue of Allegany Magazine.*

# Celebrating 200 years of the National Road

Two hundred years ago, Western Maryland was the American frontier. With a sparse population spread throughout hills and valleys and only rarely clustered in cities, the Appalachian Mountains formed a mental, if not physical, border to the United States.

Yet, the land beyond the mountains to the Mississippi River was also part of the United States. It represented an untapped source for food, lumber and fur and with barely one million Americans living on the frontier, it was ripe with opportunities.

So in May 1811, construction began on America's first federal public works project a national road that would make it easier for settlers to move into the western United States.

"The road opened up the U.S., west of the Ohio (River), which allowed the federal government to sell property it owned. There was no income tax, so a revenue source was important," said Steve Colby with the Cumberland Road Alliance. The alliance is a collaborative effort among many of the communities and businesses along the National Road to reintroduce it to public.

The National Road began in Cumberland at "a stone at the corner of lot Number One in Cumberland, near the confluence of Will's Creek and the north branch of the Potomac River," according to historical records. The road reached Wheeling, W. Va., in 1818 and Vandalia,

Ohio, in 1839.

Colby said the reason for choosing Cumberland was because, "It was a somewhat central location which both the north and south could agree on. Philadelphia was the primary port for shipping goods and the south worried about Pennsylvania's dominance as the port for shipment of western goods. Maryland was in the process of building turnpikes to Cumberland which would complete the Road to the coast."

Toll gate house of the Cumberland Road Built in 1812
6 miles west of Cumberland, Md. U.S. 40

**Construction on the National Road began in 1812 in Cumberland. Toll houses like the one in LaVale used the collected tolls to maintain the road. Courtesy of the Albert and Angela Feldstein Collection.**

Cumberland also sat next to a natural break in the mountains that made the first part of the journey a little easier.

Building the National Road from Cumberland helped establish the city as a transportation hub. Eventually, the C&O Canal would terminate there and the B&O Railroad would set up major operations there.

Colby also credits the National Road with growing Baltimore into a large port city. "Without it, Philadelphia would have continued dominance due to Pennsylvania's push to improve the Forbes Road to Pittsburgh," Colby said.

The National Road will celebrate its bicentennial on May 8, 2011.

Cumberland will host a groundbreaking and dedication of a 12-foot-tall memorial and sealed time capsule on the site where the National Road began. New interpretive signage will also be put up along the road. This will complement the original marker, which is rarely visited because it is usually not seen on the small traffic island where it is located. The new marker will be in Riverside Park where George Washington's frontier headquarters cabin is also located and only a few dozen feet from the original marker.

Steve Umling, a planner with the City of Cumberland, said that planners, historians and museums from Maryland, West Virginia and Pennsylvania are working to put together other events during the bicentennial year, such as bus trips, a black tie ball and antique car parades. All of the events are being coordinated to happen during a multistate planning conference that will also be held in Cumberland during the first week of May.

Umling said it's important to remember the anniversary because, "The National Road was the start of the federal highway program."

Various contractors built the road in small sections of a few miles each under the supervision of David Shriver, Jr., who had experience building Maryland turnpikes. However, once built, the federal government did a poor job of maintaining the road. Control of the road was eventually turned over to the states. The states erected toll gates and collected revenue to maintain the road. One of the last remaining toll houses is located only a few miles west of Cumberland.

Once built, the road has also been rerouted from time to time at several locations. The original route through Cumberland ran up Greene Street and Braddock Road, but it was rerouted in 1834 along its current route as U.S. Route 40.

You can find historic photos and documents of the National Road at Cumberland Road Alliance web site *www.cumberlandroadproject.com.*

*This article originally appeared in the Maryland Life June 2011 issue.*

# About the author

James Rada, Jr. is the author of seven novels, a non-fiction book and a non-fiction collection. These include the historical novels *Canawlers, October Mourning, Between Rail and River* and *The Rain Man.* His other novels are *Logan's Fire, Beast* and *My Little Angel.* His non-fiction books are *Battlefield Angels: The Daughters of Charity Work as Civil War Nurses* and *Looking Back: True Stories of Mountain Maryland.*

He lives in Gettysburg, Pa., where he works as a freelance writer. Jim has received numerous awards from the Maryland-Delaware-DC Press Association, Associated Press, Maryland State Teachers Association and Community Newspapers Holdings, Inc. for his newspaper writing.

If you would like to be kept up to date on new books being published by James or ask him questions, he can be reached by e-mail at *jimrada@yahoo.com.*

To see James' other books or to order copies on-line, go to *www.aimpublishinggroup.com.*

# If you liked
# LOOKING BACK,
## you can *look forward*
## to more stories at these
## FREE sites from James Rada

---

## AIM PUBLISHING GROUP
### *www.aimpublishinggroup.com*
The official web site for James Rada, Jr.'s books and news including a complete catalog of all his books (including eBooks) with ordering links. You'll also find free history articles, news and special offers.

---

## TIME WILL TELL
### *historyarchive.wordpress.com*
Read history articles by James Rada, Jr. plus other history news, pictures and trivia.

---

## WHISPERS IN THE WIND
### *jimrada.wordpress.com*
Discover more about the writing life and keep up to date on news about James Rada, Jr.